INSIGHT FOR LIVING

—————— Broadcast Schedule ——————

Changing Wanderers into Worshipers
May 9–July 8, 2002

Thursday	May 9	**A New Beginning—Worth Waiting For** Exodus 12:29–36, 40–42
Friday	May 10	**A New Beginning—Worth Waiting For**
Monday	May 13	**Unusual Leading, Remarkable Results** Exodus 13:17–14:31
Tuesday	May 14	**Unusual Leading, Remarkable Results**
Wednesday	May 15	**Unusual Leading, Remarkable Results**
Thursday	May 16	**From Eagles' Wings to Hornets' Stings** Exodus 19:1–20; 23:20–33
Friday	May 17	**From Eagles' Wings to Hornets' Stings**
Monday	May 20	**Generosity: Willing Hearts, Stirred Within** Selections from Exodus 25–36
Tuesday	May 21	**Generosity: Willing Hearts, Stirred Within**
Wednesday	May 22	**Generosity: Willing Hearts, Stirred Within**
Thursday	May 23	**Investing in Things Eternal . . . Being Blessed** Selections from Exodus 38–40
Friday	May 24	**Investing in Things Eternal . . . Being Blessed**
Monday	May 27	**Priority One: Taking God Very Seriously** Selections from Leviticus and Numbers
Tuesday	May 28	**Priority One: Taking God Very Seriously**
Wednesday	May 29	**Priority One: Taking God Very Seriously**
Thursday	May 30	**It's Time to Celebrate—Not Complain** Numbers 10:11–17; 11:1–6; 12:1–4, 9–10
Friday	May 31	**It's Time to Celebrate—Not Complain**
Monday	June 3	**It's Time to Celebrate—Not Complain**
Tuesday	June 4	**How to Fail—in Four Simple Lessons** Selections from Numbers 13 and 14
Wednesday	June 5	**How to Fail—in Four Simple Lessons**
Thursday	June 6	**How to Fail—in Four Simple Lessons**
Friday	June 7	**When a Leader Fails** Numbers 20:1–13, 23–29

Monday	June 10	**When a Leader Fails**
Tuesday	June 11	**When a Leader Fails**
Wednesday	June 12	**Same Song, Eleventh Verse . . . Hope Beyond Snakebite** Numbers 21:4–9; John 3:14–16
Thursday	June 13	**Same Song, Eleventh Verse . . . Hope Beyond Snakebite**
Friday	June 14	**Same Song, Eleventh Verse . . . Hope Beyond Snakebite**
Monday	June 17	**Almost Home** Deuteronomy 6:1–13
Tuesday	June 18	**Almost Home**
Wednesday	June 19	**How to Kick-Start a Whole New Beginning** Joshua 1:1–9
Thursday	June 20	**How to Kick-Start a Whole New Beginning**
Friday	June 21	**How to Kick-Start a Whole New Beginning**
Monday	June 24	**Watching Those Walls Tumble Down** Selections from Joshua 6
Tuesday	June 25	**Watching Those Walls Tumble Down**
Wednesday	June 26	**Defeat on the Heels of Victory** Selections from Joshua 7
Thursday	June 27	**Defeat on the Heels of Victory**
Friday	June 28	**Defeat on the Heels of Victory**
Monday	July 1	**The Secret: An Attitude of Fortitude** Joshua 14:6–14
Tuesday	July 2	**The Secret: An Attitude of Fortitude**
Wednesday	July 3	**The Secret: An Attitude of Fortitude**
Thursday	July 4	**Grace and Truth Worth Remembering** Joshua 24:1–28
Friday	July 5	**Grace and Truth Worth Remembering**
Monday	July 8	**Grace and Truth Worth Remembering**

Broadcast schedule is subject to change without notice.

Insight for Living • Post Office Box 269000, Plano, TX 75026-9000
Insight for Living Ministries • Post Office Box 2510, Vancouver, BC, V6B 3W7
Insight for Living, Inc. • 20 Albert Street, Blackburn, VIC 3130, Australia
www.insight.org
Printed in the United States of America

CHANGING WANDERERS INTO WORSHIPERS

From the Exodus
—— *to the* ——
Promised Land

Insight for Living Bible Study Guide

From the Bible-Teaching Ministry of

Charles R. Swindoll

INSIGHT FOR LIVING

Insight for Living's Bible teacher, Chuck Swindoll, has devoted his life to the clear, practical application of God's Word and His grace. A pastor at heart, Chuck has served as senior pastor to congregations in Texas, Massachusetts, and California. He currently leads Stonebriar Community Church in Frisco, Texas, but Chuck's listening audience extends far beyond a local church body. As a leading program in Christian broadcasting, *Insight for Living* airs in major Christian radio markets, through more than 2,100 outlets worldwide, in 16 languages, and to a growing webcast audience. Chuck's extensive writing ministry has also served the body of Christ worldwide, and his leadership as president and now chancellor of Dallas Theological Seminary has helped prepare and equip a new generation for ministry. Chuck and Cynthia, his partner in life and ministry, have four grown children and ten grandchildren.

Based on the outlines, charts, and transcripts of Charles R. Swindoll's sermons, the study guide text was developed and written by the Pastoral Ministries Department of Insight for Living.

Editor in Chief:
Cynthia Swindoll

Study Guide Writer:
Brian Goins

Senior Editor and Assistant Writer:
Wendy Peterson

Editor and Assistant Writer:
Marla DeShong

Editor:
Amy LaFuria

Rights and Permissions:
The Meredith Agency

Typesetter:
Bob Haskins

Unless otherwise identified, all Scripture references are from the New American Standard Bible, © The Lockman Foundation 1960, 1962, 1963, 1968, 1971, 1972, 1973, 1975, 1977, 1995. Used by permission. Scripture taken from the Holy Bible, New International Version, Copyright © 1973, 1978, 1984 International Bible Society, used by permission of Zondervan Bible Publishers [NIV]. Scripture quotations from THE MESSAGE © 1993, 1994, 1995 by Eugene H. Peterson. Used by permission of NavPress Publishing Group. Other translations cited are the King James Version [KJV], the New King James Version [NKJV], the New Living Translation [NLT], and the New Testament in Modern English [PHILLIPS].

An effort has been made to locate sources and obtain permission where necessary for the quotations used in this book. In the event of any unintentional omission, a modification will gladly be incorporated in future printings.

ISBN 1-57972-378-0
Cover design: Alex Pasieka
Cover image: Copyright © Dave Bartruff/CORBIS
Printed in the United States of America

CONTENTS

INTRODUCTION

Imagine wandering in a desert wilderness for forty years—eating the same food every day, wearing the same clothes, continually walking but going nowhere. Now add to that trying to lead two million people on this journey, most of them complaining!

Moses faced this challenge as the one appointed by the Lord God to lead the Israelites out of bondage in the land of Egypt. Lovingly, God sent manna from heaven. Powerfully, He routed Israel's enemies. Faithfully, He provided a cloud by day and a pillar of fire by night to guide His people on their journey through the desert. Yet the Hebrews possessed faithless, hard hearts that would rather worship a golden calf than acknowledge the one true God. As a result, they were often punished along the way for their disobedience.

Israel's wanderings in the wilderness would have been tragic if not for God's mercy and the leadership of a few godly men who displayed faith and grace under pressure. As you read on, you will begin to discern the strengths as well as the shortcomings of extraordinary leaders like Moses, Aaron, Joshua, and Caleb. And you will begin to see the "big picture" of God's plan for His people as you study how He transformed His complaining wanderers into reverent worshipers and led them into the Promised Land.

Charles R. Swindoll

PUTTING TRUTH
INTO ACTION

K nowledge apart from application falls short of God's desire for
His children. He wants us to apply what we learn so that we
will change and grow. This Bible study guide was prepared with
these goals in mind. As you go through the following pages, we
hope your desire to discover biblical truth will grow as your understanding of God's Word increases and that you will be encouraged
to apply what you've learned.

To assist you in your study, we've included a section called
Living Insights at the end of each lesson. These exercises will
challenge you to study further and to think of specific ways to put
your discoveries into action.

Each Living Insights section is followed an ✝ **Invitation to
Worship**, which is designed to help you examine your own heart
and lift your eyes to the Lord—as He changes you from a wanderer
into a worshiper.

There are many ways to use this guide—in personal devotions,
group studies, discussions with friends and family, and Sunday school
classes. And, of course, it's an ideal study aid when you're listening
to its corresponding *Insight for Living* radio series.

To benefit most from this Bible study guide, we encourage you
to consider it a spiritual journal. That's why we've included space
in the Living Insights for recording your thoughts and discoveries.
We hope you'll return to those sections often for review and encouragement as you continue to grow in your walk with Christ.

Insight for Living

CHANGING WANDERERS INTO WORSHIPERS

From the Exodus
―――― *to the* ――――
Promised Land

Chapter 1

A NEW BEGINNING
WORTH WAITING FOR

Exodus 12:29–36, 40–42

Dead . . . the empire was nearly dead. The once beautiful and mighty Egypt, the queen of all the earth, lay beaten and battered, nearly broken under nine plagues inflicted by her slaves' God. But it was for those very slaves—the Hebrews—that all this had taken place.

Out of their oppressors' rubble, the Hebrews would build a new life—one planned, designed, and orchestrated by the Lord Almighty!

First, however, the Lord had to bring His people through the tenth, and tragically final, plague. As the Lord had instructed them, the Hebrews stood outside the doors of their shanties and lean-tos in Goshen, daubing lambs' blood on their doorposts with bunches of hyssop. Door after door, street after street, they obeyed God's command. Because at midnight, the angel of death would come and kill all the firstborn in Egypt. Only the households covered by the blood would be spared. So the Israelites smeared the blood over their doors . . . and waited.

This harrowing night is where we begin our study of how God turned the Hebrews from wanderers to worshipers. Here God's people first stepped out in faith as a nation and began to learn what a life of worship was all about. And here is where we join them—to walk with them as God led them from the land of their enslavement to the Promised Land. We'll glory in their victories and learn from their mistakes. And we'll meet their God, for He is our God as well. So let's go back in time to that night, to wait with God's people as they stood on the verge of a new beginning.

A New Beginning

More than four hundred years before this Passover night, God had promised Abraham that He would free his descendants from slavery (see Gen. 15:13–14; Ex. 12:40–41). The Hebrews did not usher in the fulfillment of this ancient promise with shouts of joy, however, because all around them, cries of mourning rang out in the streets:

> Pharaoh arose in the night, he and all his servants and all the Egyptians, and there was a great cry in Egypt, for there was no home where there was not someone dead. (Ex. 12:30)

This was more than even Pharaoh could stand. With his own firstborn dead and the whole land wailing in grief, Pharaoh finally summoned Moses and Aaron back into his presence:

> Then he called for Moses and Aaron at night and said, "Rise up, get out from among my people, both you and the sons of Israel; and go, worship the Lord, as you have said. Take both your flocks and your herds, as you have said, and go, and bless me also." [1] (Ex. 12:31–32)

What suffering Pharaoh had put himself and his people through! Perhaps the Egyptians still bore marks from the boils and insect stings that had been inflicted upon them. For certain, they still nursed the mental and emotional scars of seeing their land and lives destroyed before their eyes. So Pharaoh finally relented, and his people echoed his bitter dismissal of the Hebrews from the land:

> The Egyptians urged the people to hurry and leave the country. "For otherwise," they said, "we will all die!" (v. 33 NIV)

The slaughter of their firstborn children was overwhelming. While the Egyptians cradled their dead, the Hebrews embarked on

---

1. Pharaoh's request, "Bless me also," seems sincere, not sarcastic. Despite his unrepentant heart, he acknowledged God's power and wished that God would use that power to help him now. See Brevard S. Childs, *The Book of Exodus: A Critical, Theological Commentary,* The Old Testament Library Commentary Series (Louisville, Ky.: Westminster Press, 1974), p. 183; and Walter C. Kaiser, Jr., "Exodus," in *The Expositor's Bible Commentary,* ed. Frank E. Gaebelein (Grand Rapids, Mich.: Zondervan Publishing House, 1990), vol. 2, p. 377.

a new life of freedom. Along with their food and belongings, they brought articles of silver and gold and clothing that had belonged to the Egyptians (vv. 34–36). It was the Lord's plan that the nation which had enslaved and plundered His people would in turn be plundered by Israel (see 3:21–22; 11:2; 12:36b). The once-oppressed Hebrews left the land as a conquering army would—with booty in hand and leaving nothing of worth behind.

With new treasures, their own possessions, and their cattle, the Hebrews gathered in Rameses and headed to a place called Succoth, where Moses counted about six hundred thousand men; the total of this "mixed multitude" may have numbered around two million (vv. 37–38).[2] Imagine—it would be like the entire city of Paris picking up and moving out of France! This journey from slavery to freedom was something the Israelites would never forget:

> Now the time that the sons of Israel lived in Egypt was four hundred and thirty years. And at the end of four hundred and thirty years, to the very day, all the hosts of the Lord went out from the land of Egypt. (Ex. 12:40–41)

To help His people call this sacred event to mind for all time, God instructed Moses to institute a holy day. In fact, the Hebrew year would now begin with the month of their departure as a permanent recollection of their new beginning (v. 2). And this holy day with its holy feast was to be the centerpiece of this special month. As Moses wrote:

> Because the Lord kept vigil that night to bring them out of Egypt, on this night all the Israelites are to keep vigil to honor the Lord for the generations to come. (v. 42 NIV)

A New Observance

The rest of Exodus 12 and most of chapter 13 record the Lord's instructions for the Hebrews' new observance, the Passover. All of God's covenant people, and only God's covenant people, were to take part in it. If a foreign-born man wanted to celebrate the Passover, he had to be circumcised in accordance with God's covenant

---

2. See Kaiser, "Exodus," p. 379.

with Abraham (vv. 43–45, 47–49; see also Gen. 17:12–14). God also instructed, prophetically, that none of the sacrificial lambs' bones were to be broken (Ex. 12:46; see also Ps. 22:17; John 19:31–33).

In chapter 13, the Lord added to the Passover the Feast of Unleavened Bread and the consecration of the firstborn. Let's explore these instructions to the Israelites and see what truths we can glean from them for our day.

Observing and Keeping

Let's take a closer look at God's instructions regarding the Feast of Unleavened Bread:

> Moses said to the people, "Remember this day in which you went out of Egypt, from the house of slavery; for by a powerful hand the Lord brought you out from this place. And nothing leavened shall be eaten. On this day, in the month of Abib, you are about to go forth. It shall be when the Lord brings you to the land of the Canaanite, the Hittite, the Amorite, the Hivite and the Jebusite, which He swore to your fathers to give you, a land flowing with milk and honey, that you shall *observe* this rite in this month. . . . Therefore, you shall *keep* this ordinance at its appointed time from year to year." (13:3–5, 10, emphasis added)

The Lord directed the Hebrews to eat bread without yeast during the week prior to the climactic Passover feast (vv. 6–7a). Not even a speck of yeast was to be seen in their camp (v. 7b)![3] The Lord designed this observance as a "sign" and "reminder" of what He had done for them in Egypt (vv. 8–10). He wanted them to "observe" and "keep" this rite—to mark it on their calendars and make it the annual symbol of their identity as His people.

In this feast God instituted a powerful observance in which Israel would remember and reenact His love for them throughout their lives. The Hebrews may have thought that their freedom was an end in itself, but to God it was only the beginning. He had a

---

3. In the Bible, leaven, or yeast, symbolizes evil. Through the removing of all traces of leaven from their households, the Israelites learned that they must separate themselves from sin in order to commune with God. See Maxie Dunham, "Exodus," in *The Communicator's Commentary*, ed. Lloyd J. Ogilvie (Waco, Tex.: Word Books, 1987), vol. 2, p. 152.

specific purpose in mind, as He would tell His people later:

> "'If you will indeed obey My voice and keep My covenant, then you shall be My own possession among all the peoples, for all the earth is Mine; and you shall be to Me a kingdom of priests and a holy nation.'" (19:5–6a)

Devoting

God also told the Hebrews to "sanctify," or "devote," to Him their male firstborn—both human and animal:

> "Sanctify to Me every firstborn, the first offspring of every womb among the sons of Israel, both of man and beast; it belongs to Me." (13:2)

> "You shall devote to the Lord the first offspring of every womb, and the first offspring of every beast that you own; the males belong to the Lord." (13:12)

Animals were to be sacrificed, but human beings were, of course, "consecrated to the Lord by their life, not by their death."[4] For certain animals on which the Israelites' lives depended and for their children, substitutes could be made. Every firstborn donkey, for example, could be redeemed by a lamb sacrificed in its place, and every firstborn boy could also be redeemed by a lamb (Ex. 13:13).

Why did the Lord institute this observance? Because He purchased the Hebrews' freedom with the death of all the firstborn of Egypt *and* the slaughtering of hundreds of thousands of animals (vv. 14–15). But He redeemed Israel, whom He called His firstborn son (see 4:22). Likewise, the Hebrews were instructed to redeem their firstborn sons, honoring the mercy the Lord had shown them.

Telling

Did you notice a couple of recurring phrases in Exodus 13:1–16? Look at verses 8 and 14:

> "You shall *tell* your son on that day, saying, 'It is because of what the Lord did for me and when I came out of Egypt.'" (v. 8, emphasis added)

---

4. Ronald Youngblood and Walter C. Kaiser Jr., note on Exodus 13:13, *The NIV Study Bible*, ed. Kenneth L. Barker (Grand Rapids, Mich.: Zondervan Bible Publishers, 1985), p. 105.

"And it shall be when your son asks you in time to come, saying, 'What is this?' then you shall *say* to him, 'With a powerful hand the Lord brought us out of Egypt, from the house of slavery.'" (v. 14, emphasis added)

To ensure that successive generations would know of His grace and power displayed at the Exodus, the Lord instructed the Hebrews to communicate to their children the significance of the celebration. This verbal interplay became an integral part of the Passover feast. It made the holy day not only a recollection of past deliverance, but also a "nourishment for future redemption."[5]

Observing the Feast of Unleavened Bread, devoting their firstborn, and telling future generations of God's power and grace gave the Israelites tangible ways to worship God—a natural response to the love He had shown them. Although He gave His instructions in the form of commands, they weren't a burden or drudgery. The Hebrews received them gladly because the instructions showed them how to express outwardly the thanks and joy they felt in their hearts.

Toward a New Way of Life—for Us

As they experienced freedom for the first time in centuries, the Israelites needed to learn a new way of life. Never before had they witnessed the miracles of God. Never before had they been asked to observe a rite, nor had their lives ever revolved around a sacred observance. And never before had they devoted themselves to anything but making Egyptian bricks. They needed training, so God began to show them how to become *His* people with *His* plan and priorities, to serve *His* will *His* way.

Has God brought you out of sin's destructive slavery and into the beauty of His loving freedom? Has His Passover Lamb, His firstborn Son, redeemed your life from spiritual death (see 1 Cor. 5:7b; Rev. 1:5)? If so, the feast of your salvation is the Lord's crucifixion and resurrection—*observe it!* Set aside the bunnies and baskets and reclaim Easter for the great spiritual reality it is. Read the gospel accounts, spend time with the Lord in prayer, and thank Him for His mercy and power exercised on your behalf. And remember, our feast of salvation isn't limited to one Sunday but can (and should) be celebrated throughout the year.

5. John Calvin, as quoted by Brevard Childs in *The Book of Exodus*, p. 211.

As God's redeemed person, *devote yourself to Him*! Paul taught us in Romans 12 to "present your bodies a living and holy sacrifice, acceptable to God, which is your spiritual service of worship" (v. 1). Our lives are for God's service, ready to accomplish His purposes, His way. What are some practical ways we can devote ourselves to Him? We can:

- devote ourselves to prayer (Acts 1:14; 6:4; Rom. 12:12; 1 Cor. 7:5; Col. 4:2)

- devote ourselves to learning and teaching God's Word (Acts 2:42; 6:4; 18:5)

- devote ourselves to serving others (1 Cor. 16:15; 1 Tim. 5:10)

- devote ourselves to loving one another (Rom. 12:10)

Then, as the Lord's redeemed and consecrated people, we can *tell others the Good News*! And we can start with our children, just as the Israelites did. The Light we've been given wasn't meant to be hidden "under a basket" but set high to shine clear and strong, drawing people to the Giver of light (Matt. 5:14–16).

As believers, we have a lot in common with God's chosen people of old; like them, we are "a chosen race, a royal priesthood, a holy nation, a people for God's own possession, so that [we] may proclaim the excellencies of Him who has called [us] out of darkness into His marvelous light" (1 Pet. 2:9). And from the Hebrews, we can learn a lot about walking with our Lord.

As we travel with the ancient Israelites, we'll discover that God has a plan for us too. He wants to enrich our own worship of Him, to fill us with hope for our future by showing us what He's done for His people in the past. He wants to bring us into His presence so that we can see His face . . . and His heart. He wants to give us a deeper reservoir of experience from which to draw, so that we can saturate our worship with a greater knowledge of His character and concern for us.

So let's join the Lord and His people and let the adventure begin!

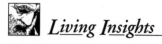 *Living Insights*

As the Hebrews hid in their homes during the Passover, they could not have known that their blood-smeared doorposts prefigured a future and even greater act of God's salvation—the blood-soaked timbers of the cross. As they ate the lamb, they surely didn't know that a man, the Lamb of God, would one day be slaughtered for the sins of the world.

That Lamb of God was Jesus Christ, who died for us. He purchased our freedom by shedding His blood. He was, and is, "our Passover" (1 Cor. 5:7). Author Max Lucado describes the kind of Passover Lamb Christ became on our behalf:

> After generations of people had spit on his face, he still loved them. After a nation of chosen ones had stripped him naked and ripped his incarnated flesh, he still died for them. And even today, after billions have chosen to prostitute themselves before the pimps of power, fame, and wealth, he still waits for them.[6]

Are you observing Christ's presence in your life with the same sense of importance and vigilance that the Hebrews celebrated the Passover? If so, how?

_____

_____

_____

_____

What do you do to dedicate, or devote, yourself to Him regularly?

_____

_____

_____

_____

6. Max Lucado, *God Came Near: Chronicles of the Christ* (Portland, Ore.: Multnomah Press, 1987), p. 33.

If you feel you need some improvement in these areas, write out your ideas.

_____

_____

_____

_____

_____

_____

Now go to Christ in prayer. Praise Him for being the Savior of the world. Thank Him for saving you. And dedicate yourself to loving Him and walking with Him for the rest of your days.

 ## *Invitation to Worship*

> O magnify the Lord with me,
> And let us exalt His name together. (Ps. 34:3)

The goal of this study is not simply to gain information about the Hebrews, but to grow in our own worship of God. So at the end of each chapter, we'll include an Invitation to Worship. Whatever flash of inspiration each episode in the Hebrews' lives brings, let it prompt you to give praise and thanksgiving to the Lord for what He's doing in your life. Consider His ways, how He lavishes His people with love, patience, grace, and refining fire—all for our own spiritual growth. Let yourself be full of awe and wonder at the Lord's power and love.

When Christians take Communion, we, too, are recalling the deliverance God accomplished for us. Our enslavement was sin; our taskmaster, Satan. But at the price of His only Son, Jesus Christ, the Lord redeemed us and won our freedom, and we now walk with Him as He leads us to our Promised Land, heaven. Along the way, like the Hebrews, we need to stop regularly and remember what God has done for us. For the Hebrews, that time of remembrance was the Passover. We recall our Easter triumph in Communion.

The next time you sit or kneel to take the bread and wine, remember when God set you free, when He first brought you to faith in His Son—your personal Passover. Praise Him for His power to raise Jesus Christ from the dead. Thank Him for using that power to give you new life. Let those remembrances infuse your heart with hope and fill your thoughts with the knowledge that you'll one day spend eternity with Him in heaven.

Now take time to pray. We'll get you started with some thoughts, but you're invited to complete the prayer, bringing your own thoughts, feelings, burdens, petitions, intercessions, and praises to the Lord.

> *Dear Lamb of God,*
>
> *Thank you for giving Yourself to be slain in my place. I praise you for imprisoning Yourself in a fleshly body so that my spirit could soar free. As I think of You on the cross, I fall to my knees in humble thanksgiving. Thank You for being pierced for my transgressions and crushed for my iniquities. Thank You that in Your blood I may find protection and in Your wounds find healing.*
>
> *I pray that the thought of the blood-soaked timbers of Your cross would remind me of how You saved me from spiritual death, just the way You saved the Hebrews who had blood-smeared doorposts. Grant me grace, O Lord, that I would never forget the price You paid to save me, to make me one of Your own, to call me out and lead me into righteousness.*
>
> *Give me the strength now, Lord, as I continue in my journey. Stand by me so that I can face the challenges that await me. Help me as I seek to . . .*

Chapter 2

UNUSUAL LEADING, REMARKABLE RESULTS

Exodus 13:17–14:31

D id you notice something the Lord told Moses again and again in Exodus 13?

> "Remember this day . . . for by a powerful hand the Lord brought you out from this place." (v. 3)

> "For with a powerful hand the Lord brought you out of Egypt." (v. 9b)

> "And it shall be when your son asks . . . then you shall say to him, 'With a powerful hand the Lord brought us out of Egypt, from the house of slavery.'" (v. 14)

> "For with a powerful hand the Lord brought us out of Egypt." (v. 16b)

With a powerful hand the Lord brought plagues that destroyed the pride of Egypt. *With a powerful hand* He took the lives of merciless Egypt's firstborn. *With a powerful hand* He spared His people from every grief He inflicted on their Egyptian oppressors. *With a powerful hand* He led His people out of slavery and started them toward a new life of freedom.

Incredibly, even after all these miracles, the Lord had only *begun* to show His might! As we'll see in the next passages from Exodus, the Lord's powerful hand would free the Hebrews from Egypt's defiant grasp once and for all. And He would do it in a way that no one had ever considered.

God's Unusual Leading

Two routes would have taken the Israelites directly from Egypt

Parts of this chapter have been adapted from "Between the Devil and the Deep Red Sea" in the Bible study guide *Moses: A Man of Selfless Dedication*, written by Jason Shepherd, from the Bible-teaching ministry of Charles R. Swindoll (Anaheim, Calif.: Charles R. Swindoll, Inc., 1998).

to Canaan. The first road, "the way of the land of the Philistines" (Ex. 13:17), ran east out of Goshen and hugged the coast of the Mediterranean Sea all the way to the northern part of the Promised Land. The second route, the way to Shur, also blazed an easterly trail into the desert, parallel to the Philistine way, to the southern border of Canaan.

The Lord chose neither of these paths for His people:

> Now when Pharaoh had let the people go, God did not lead them by the way of the land of the Philistines, even though it was near; for God said, "The people might change their minds when they see war, and return to Egypt." Hence God led the people around by the way of the wilderness to the Red Sea; and the sons of Israel went up in martial array from the land of Egypt. Moses took the bones of Joseph with him, for he had made the sons of Israel solemnly swear, saying, "God will surely take care of you, and you shall carry my bones from here with you." Then they set out from Succoth and camped in Etham on the edge of the wilderness. (vv. 17–20)

Why did the Lord have Moses take the people south, deep into the desert? One of these reasons, as verse 17 shows, is that the Lord didn't want His people to be frightened away from freedom by enemy attacks.[1] In addition, God knew that they needed to grow in their trust and knowledge of Him. To build their faith, the Lord would put them in a situation from which they could find deliverance only in His power and protection, only by a miracle of His making. He led them there in a unique and sovereign way:

> The Lord was going before them in a pillar of cloud by day to lead them on the way, and in a pillar of fire by night to give them light, that they might travel by day and by night. He did not take away the pillar of cloud by day, nor the pillar of fire by night, from before the people. (Ex. 12:21–22)

---

1. According to John I. Durham, "There was a well-fortified military road on the direct route from the Egyptian Delta into Canaan." *Word Biblical Commentary: Exodus* (Waco, Tex.: Word Books, 1987), vol. 3, p. 185. See also Brevard S. Childs, *The Book of Exodus: A Critical, Theological Commentary*, The Old Testament Library Series (Philadelphia, Pa.: Westminster Press, 1974), p. 229.

With His own guiding presence, God led the Israelites south to an outpost town named Etham, "on the edge of the wilderness" (v. 20). The Hebrews made camp on the edge of the desert, on the edge of fear, on the edge of something remarkable.

God's Underlying Purpose

At Etham, God met with Moses and told him where to lead the people next—to the Bermuda Triangle of the wilderness (14:1–2)! On one side would be the desert; on another, Egypt; and on the third, the sea. If Pharaoh changed his mind and came after them, they would be trapped. There was no way of escape; the Egyptian army would wipe them off the face of the earth. But the Lord had a different plan in mind.

God's Plans

God told Moses:

> "Pharaoh will say of the sons of Israel, 'They are wandering aimlessly in the land; the wilderness has shut them in.' Thus I will harden Pharaoh's heart, and he will chase after them; and I will be honored through Pharaoh and all his army, and the Egyptians will know that I am the Lord." And they did so. (vv. 3–4)

Bible scholar John Durham notes that "this route is given for a theological reason, as is nearly all the information in Exodus. . . . Yahweh determined the route as a ruse by which he might get further glory at Pharaoh's expense."[2] Do you remember what Pharaoh had initially told Moses when he had asked the ruler to let the people go? "Who is the Lord that I should obey His voice to let Israel go? I do not know the Lord" (Ex. 5:2a). He would soon know beyond a doubt who Yahweh was and why all glory, honor, and obedience belonged to Him.

Pharaoh's Response

Just as the Lord predicted, Pharaoh assembled his army and pursued the Israelites:

> When the king of Egypt was told that the people

2. Durham, *Word Biblical Commentary: Exodus*, p. 185.

had fled, Pharaoh and his servants had a change of heart toward the people, and they said, "What is this we have done, that we have let Israel go from serving us?" (14:5)

Taking with him "six hundred select chariots, and all the other chariots of Egypt with officers over all of them" (v. 7), Pharaoh and his army thundered over the horizon. And all the Hebrews could do was watch them come.

The Hebrews' Panic

Terrified by the sight of the approaching army, the Hebrews cried out to the Lord to rescue them (v. 10). All too quickly, however, their fear turned to angry blame, with Moses as their target:

> Then they said to Moses, "Is it because there were no graves in Egypt that you have taken us away to die in the wilderness? Why have you dealt with us in this way, bringing us out of Egypt? Is this not the word that we spoke to you in Egypt, saying, 'Leave us alone that we may serve the Egyptians'? For it would have been better for us to serve the Egyptians than to die in the wilderness." (vv. 11–12)

Even after experiencing the Lord's power and protection in Egypt, the people still didn't trust Him. Instead, they yearned for the familiar, even if it was familiar misery. Five times they pointed back to Egypt, as if to say, "Being slaves and having our babies killed wasn't *that* bad!" (see Ex. 1).[3] But Moses shored up their shaky faith by turning their eyes away from Pharaoh's army and toward the Lord:

> Moses said to the people, "Do not fear! Stand by and see the salvation of the Lord which *He will accomplish for you* today; for the Egyptians whom you have seen today, you will never see them again forever. *The Lord will fight for you* while you keep silent." (Ex. 14:13–14, emphasis added)

---

3. Brevard S. Childs observes that "the parallel in vocabulary between Israel's reaction and the Egyptians when hearing of Israel's escape is striking: 'What is this we have done that we have let Israel go from serving us?' // 'What is this you have done to us . . . in bringing us out of Egypt? . . . better to serve them.' The two reactions are parallel because neither reckoned with God's plan." *The Book of Exodus*, pp. 225–26.

"Don't give in to fear," Moses told them, "but watch what the Lord will do—and keep quiet!" It was time to hush their panic and to watch the Lord act, for He would free them from their enemy once and for all.

God's Remarkable Deliverance

Though he trusted the Lord, Moses didn't know His plans either. Perhaps he asked the Lord for guidance or complained about the Hebrews' lack of faith, which would explain why the Lord told him to quit "crying out to Me" and lead the people forward (v. 15). The miracle was about to happen, and God wanted to explain Moses' part in it:

> "As for you, lift up your staff and stretch out your hand over the sea and divide it, and the sons of Israel shall go through the midst of the sea on dry land." (v. 16)

Then He explained what He would be doing, echoing the theme of honor He had spoken of earlier (see v. 4):

> "As for Me, behold, I will harden the hearts of the Egyptians so that they will go in after them; and I will be honored through Pharaoh and all his army, through his chariots and his horsemen. Then the Egyptians will know that I am the Lord, when I am honored through Pharaoh, through his chariots and his horsemen." (vv. 17–18)

His Power Displayed

The first step in the Lord's plan was to protect His people by preventing the Egyptians from pursuing them any farther:

> The angel of God, who had been going before the camp of Israel, moved and went behind them; and the pillar of cloud moved from before them and stood behind them. So it came between the camp of Egypt and the camp of Israel; and there was the cloud along with the darkness, yet it gave light at night. Thus the one did not come near the other all night. (vv. 19–20)

With His angel and the pillar of cloud running interference

15

between the Israelites and the Egyptians, the Lord created a way of escape for His people:

> Then Moses stretched out his hand over the sea;[4] and the Lord swept the sea back by a strong east wind all night and turned the sea into dry land, so the waters were divided. The sons of Israel went through the midst of the sea on the dry land, and the waters were like a wall to them on their right hand and on their left. (Ex. 14:21–22)

Notice that the sea didn't part in a few minutes so the people could cross right way, as it does in the movies! Rather, the Israelites witnessed God's protection and provision all through the night.

Their deliverance was their prideful enemy's ruin:

> Then the Egyptians took up the pursuit, and all Pharaoh's horses, his chariots and his horsemen went in after them into the midst of the sea. At the morning watch, the Lord looked down on the army of the Egyptians through the pillar of fire and cloud and brought the army of the Egyptians into confusion. He caused their chariot wheels to swerve, and He made them drive with difficulty; so the Egyptians said, "Let us flee from Israel, for the Lord is fighting for them against the Egyptians." (vv. 23–25)

Not understanding what the parted sea meant and who was behind it, the Egyptian army rushed between the walls of water after the Israelites. Amazingly, they still thought they could prevail and recapture their fleeing slaves—until they came face-to-face with the power of the Lord. Their army thrown into confusion, their chariots and horses out of control, they finally recognized that a power greater than any human being was at work—and at work *against* them. Finally, the Egyptians knew the Lord. But it was too late:

> Then the Lord said to Moses, "Stretch out your hand over the sea so that the waters may come back over the Egyptians, over their chariots and their horsemen." So Moses stretched out his hand over

---

4. Moses' gesture signaled the oncoming display of the Lord's power, as well as the authority God had given him (compare Ex. 4:4; 9:22; 10:12, 21).

the sea, and the sea returned to its normal state at daybreak, while the Egyptians were fleeing right into it; then the Lord overthrew the Egyptians in the midst of the sea. The waters returned and covered the chariots and the horsemen, even Pharaoh's entire army that had gone into the sea after them; not even one of them remained. (vv. 26–28)

The pursuers fled. The conquering army was conquered. Just as his land lay in ruins, so now Pharaoh's army was destroyed, as were all of the false gods of Egypt.

With one mighty miracle, Yahweh, the Lord of heaven and earth, vanquished the most powerful army of the most powerful nation. He is always the one in charge—not Pharaoh, not wealth, not military might, not oppression, not evil. Through His indisputable triumph, the glory and honor were all His:

> But the sons of Israel walked on dry land through the midst of the sea, and the waters were like a wall to them on their right hand and on their left.
> Thus the Lord saved Israel that day from the hand of the Egyptians, and Israel saw the Egyptians dead on the seashore. When Israel saw the great power which the Lord had used against the Egyptians, the people feared the Lord, and they believed in the Lord and in His servant Moses. (vv. 29–31)

As they watched the bodies of the drowned Egyptians wash up on the shore, the Israelites bowed in reverence and fear before their all-powerful God. Then they broke forth in praise, exalting the Lord in a song of heartfelt worship (15:1–21). They had passed from slavery to freedom, from death to life, by the powerful, redeeming hand of the Lord. Life would never be the same again.

Concluding Thoughts

What can we take into our lives today from these pages of Scripture? A picture of how powerful and sovereign our Lord is. As Moses and the rescued Israelites sang,

> "Your right hand, O Lord, is majestic in power,
> Your right hand, O Lord, shatters the enemy. . . .
> Who is like You, majestic in holiness,

Awesome in praises, working wonders? . . .
In Your lovingkindness You have led the people
    whom You have redeemed;
In Your strength You have guided them to Your holy
    habitation." (15:6, 11b, 13)

In these scenes from Exodus we also see a picture of our rescue from sin and death and our deliverance to new life through God's powerful, redeeming work in His Son, Jesus Christ.

What else do you see? Take all that you can think of, follow the Israelites' lead, and praise the Lord for it, won't you? He loves to hear the joyful singing of His rescued and redeemed people!

 Living Insights

How much we have to be thankful for! Yet how often we lose sight of it, especially when we forget what we've been rescued from or when God's leading seems unusual and takes us to unsafe places.

The Israelites were certainly in a tight spot, with the desert behind them, the Egyptians hot after them, and the sea in front of them. Are you in a difficult situation right now? What's hemming you in? Finances? Unemployment? A troubled marriage? Straying children? Health problems? Grief?

_____

_____

_____

_____

_____

Sometimes God uses trials in our lives to break us of bad habits and sin patterns. Is He doing this in your situation? If so, what habits or patterns might He be asking you to change? In what ways will making these changes challenge your faith and trust in Him?

_____

_____

_____

_____

_____

_____

More than anything, the Lord wants us to know and trust Him. That's why, when we're buffeted on all sides, the only place to look is up. Unfortunately, our human tendency is to look at our problems and panic. Where are your eyes focused? How would looking up to the Lord impact your panic or despondency?

_____

_____

_____

_____

_____

_____

Do you want to glorify the Lord in your troubled situation? If you try to handle matters your own way and in your own strength, who gets the glory? How was the Lord honored in the Israelite-Egyptian situation we studied in this chapter? How can you let the Lord "fight" for you?

_____

_____

_____

_____

_____

_____

Often Christians fall into thinking that if we do W-X-Y, then the Lord will do Z. But He doesn't operate by our formulas. Just as the Israelites did not and could not do anything to get the Lord to open the Red Sea, so we can't manipulate God into solving our problems our way. "Red Seas" open and close at the Lord's command, and no one else's. He has His own methods and His own timing.

Have you been struggling against the Lord's timing? If so, in what areas? How has this affected your trust and worship of Him? What steps can you take to gain peace in these areas? How can you demonstrate your faith in God's goodness and His perfect timing?

_____

_____

_____

_____

_____

_____

Commit yourself in prayer right now to Him, His timing, and His ways. He is trustworthy (read Ps. 9:7–10), and He delights to deliver those who trust in Him (read Ps. 34:17–19; 37:23).

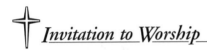 ## Invitation to Worship

> "I will sing to the Lord, for He is highly exalted;
> The horse and its rider He has hurled into the sea.
> The Lord is my strength and song,
> And He has become my salvation;
> This is my God, and I will praise Him;
> My father's God, and I will extol Him."
> (Ex. 15:1b–2)

This was how Moses and the Israelites began their song to the awesome Lord who delivered them! Take some time now to prayerfully read the rest of their song and Miriam's refrain (vv. 1–21). Then reflect on what God has done in your life. How has He blessed you? How has He delivered you? Perhaps you can begin to echo Israel's song through the following prayer:

> *Gracious Deliverer,*
> *I was trapped. My sin and my failures hemmed me*
> *in on all sides. My situation seemed hopeless.*
> *But then Your Spirit lifted my eyes up to You. You*

stood between me and those who would condemn me. You made a way of escape for me through the Cross of Christ.

Now I stand on the other side, all my sins and all the accusations of others washed away, never to return.

Dear Lord, please continue to guide me and build my faith. Help me to not give in to fear, to keep my eyes on You, to quiet my racing mind and watch You work Your miracles. Help me to believe You when . . .

_____

_____

_____

_____

_____

_____

_____

_____

_____

_____

_____

_____

_____

_____

Chapter 3

FROM EAGLES' WINGS TO HORNETS' STINGS

Exodus 19:1–20; 23:20–33

With Egypt miles behind and a mountain looming before them, the Hebrews pounded tent stakes into the ground once more. After about ninety days, this had become second nature to them. The former-slaves-turned-wandering-gypsies had moved from one campsite to the next. They had walked through a sea, traversed miles of desert, and won their first battle over the Amalekites (Ex. 14–17).

But the Hebrews wore freedom like sandals two sizes too small. They balked over bitter water (15:22–27), yearned for the food they had in captivity (16:2–3), and as the scabs from their whip-worn backs healed to scars, wondered if freedom was really worth the trouble. "Why, now," they demanded of Moses, "have you brought us up from Egypt, to kill us and our children and our livestock with thirst?" (17:3).

How did this grumbling, wandering, slave-born horde learn to handle their freedom? And, more importantly, for what purpose had God secured it?

For the next year, the Lord had the nomads stop their travels and become desert dwellers. Their calloused feet stopped throbbing; their hunger and thirst were satisfied. And they learned the purpose of their freedom—to become a unified nation and a people with a unique mission.

Rendezvous at Sinai

For four hundred years, the Israelites' productivity dictated their value in Egyptian eyes, but not in God's eyes. Now Yahweh wanted them to become a new people—no longer slaves of a tyrant, but servants of the King of Kings. To accomplish this, He taught them about their new identity and their new way of life . . . and about the God who was calling them to Himself.

The Lord then brought them to Sinai, which is also known in Scripture as Horeb, "the mountain of God" (Ex. 3:1). This is where Yahweh had first revealed Himself to Moses in the burning bush, telling Moses the secret of His name—"I am who I am" (v. 14), the ever-present, ever-living, ever-caring God—and promising deliverance and a beautiful future for His afflicted people:

> "I have surely seen the affliction of My people who are in Egypt, and have given heed to their cry because of their taskmasters, for I am aware of their sufferings. So I have come down to deliver them from the power of the Egyptians, and to bring them up from that land to a good and spacious land, to a land flowing with milk and honey." (vv. 7–8a)

Yahweh had even given Moses a guarantee:

> "Certainly I will be with you, and this shall be the sign to you that it is I who have sent you: when you have brought the people out of Egypt, you shall worship God at this mountain." (v. 12)

And now Moses and the freed people were there:

> In the third month after the sons of Israel had gone out of the land of Egypt, on that very day they came into the wilderness of Sinai. . . . and there Israel camped in front of the mountain. (19:1, 2b)

From destruction to deliverance, God kept His promises!

The Lord's Vision for His People

As the Israelites settled in their new camp, Moses sought the Lord and His direction (v. 3a). In turn, the Lord called out to him once again from this mountain, giving a tender picture of His deliverance:

> "Thus you shall say to the house of Jacob and tell the sons of Israel: 'You yourselves have seen what I did to the Egyptians, and how I bore you on eagles' wings, and brought you to Myself.'" (vv. 3b–4; see also Deut. 32:10–12)

Commentator George A. F. Knight brings us to the heart of this picture:

> The eagle was known for its unusual devotion to its young. . . . In teaching its young to fly it carried them upon its back to those great heights

23

that overlook the plains of Sinai, then it dropped them down into the depths. If the baby was still too young and too bewildered to fly, father-eagle would swoop down beneath it, catch it on his back, and fly up again with it to the eyrie on the crags above. And that, says the divine voice, is "how I brought you out of Egypt to myself!"[1]

Notice, it's to Himself that the Lord brought them. He didn't just turn them loose and let them fend for themselves. No, He protected and guided them, bringing them close to the God of love and light.

Next, the Lord proposed a covenant with an extraordinary promise attached to it:

"'Now then, if you will indeed obey My voice and keep My covenant, then you shall be My own possession among all the peoples, for all the earth is Mine; and you shall be to Me a kingdom of priests and a holy nation.' These are the words that you shall speak to the sons of Israel." (Ex. 19:5–6)

Yahweh's "own possession," a "kingdom of priests," a "holy nation"—these were the Lord's plans for His people! He promised their *priority* and their *purity*: they would be His special treasure among all the nations, taking priority over all the villages, cities, and kingdoms of the earth; they would be the people who reflected a holy God to humanity.

This great privilege and responsibility was theirs *if* they did as the Lord instructed them: "If you will indeed obey My voice and keep My covenant, then you shall be . . ." (v. 5a).

When Moses told them the Lord's plan, the people eagerly exclaimed, "All that the Lord has spoken we will do!" (v. 8). Joyfully Moses proclaimed to the Lord that the people had agreed to the covenant. The Lord responded by promising that He would be with Moses and that He would affirm his leadership in front of the people (v. 9). Then Yahweh instructed Moses to prepare the people to meet their God and to receive the conditions of the covenant.

---

1. George A. F. Knight, *Theology as Narration: A Commentary on the Book of Exodus* (Grand Rapids, Mich.: William B. Eerdmans Publishing Co., 1976), p. 128.

The Lord's Requirements for His People

It was clear that the sovereign, almighty Lord of Israel was not to be treated lightly. On the contrary, He was to be taken very seriously:

> The Lord also said to Moses, "Go to the people and consecrate them today and tomorrow, and let them wash their garments; and let them be ready for the third day, for on the third day the Lord will come down on Mount Sinai in the sight of all the people. You shall set bounds for the people all around, saying, 'Beware that you do not go up on the mountain or touch the border of it; whoever touches the mountain shall surely be put to death.'" (vv. 10–12)

Consecrate . . . be ready . . . do not touch. Three times the Lord told Moses to warn the people not to come near the mountain when He descended on it, so they would not die (vv. 12, 21, 24). The Lord is a God of love, but He is also holy beyond our ability to comprehend. Brevard S. Childs notes: "The warning is given for the sake of the people, who have no experience as yet of the dimensions of divine holiness, and lest warned will destroy themselves." [2] The warnings tell of God's love, and the way in which He comes to the people shows His awesome, fearsome holiness:

> So it came about on the third day, when it was morning, that there were thunder and lightning flashes and a thick cloud upon the mountain and a very loud trumpet sound, so that all the people who were in the camp trembled. . . . Mount Sinai was all in smoke because the Lord descended upon it in fire; and its smoke ascended like the smoke of a furnace, and the whole mountain quaked violently. When the sound of the trumpet grew louder and louder, Moses spoke and God answered him with thunder. (Ex. 19:16, 18–19)

Yahweh thundered out His requirements for His holy people— He gave them His holy Law (Ex. 20–23), which includes the section we are most familiar with, the Ten Commandments (20:2–17). This

---

2. Brevard S. Childs, *The Book of Exodus: A Critical, Theological Commentary,* The Old Testament Library Series (Philadelphia, Pa.: Westminster Press, 1974), p. 370.

giving of the Law is "the most important event of Exodus, and even the O[ld] T[estament] itself."[3]

Brevard Childs illuminates its continuing significance:

> The covenant at Sinai remains a witness for all ages of the ultimate seriousness of God's revelation of himself and his will to the world. God comes as an act of grace to join to himself a people, but his unveiling likewise brings with it a judgment. The New Testament is fully in accord with the Old in testifying that the God made known in Jesus Christ is not different in character from the consuming fire of Sinai. His covenant claim lays hold on man to demand full commitment on the central issue of life and death. Election by God brings no comfortable special status, but an invitation both to share the redemption of God to the world and to bear witness to his final judgment of sin.[4]

The Law would teach Israel's redeemed witnesses how to relate to God and to each other with truth and honor, with justice and compassion. It defined what a holy nation would look like.

When the Lord finished giving the Law to Moses, He then explained what He promised to do for such a nation.

Looking Ahead to the Promised Land

God next urged the Israelites to trust Him completely.

"I Will . . ."

> "Behold, I am going to send an angel before you to guard you along the way and to bring you into the place which I have prepared. Be on your guard before him and obey his voice; do not be rebellious toward him, for he will not pardon your transgression, since My name is in him. But if you truly obey his voice and do all that I say, then I will be an enemy to your enemies and an adversary to your

3. John I. Durham, *Word Biblical Commentary: Exodus* (Waco, Tex.: Word Books, 1987), vol. 3, p. 265.

4. Childs, *The Book of Exodus*, p. 383.

adversaries. For My angel will go before you and bring you in to the land. . . . I will send My terror ahead of you, and throw into confusion all the people among whom you come, and I will make all your enemies turn their backs to you. I will send hornets ahead of you so that they will drive out the Hivites, the Canaanites, and the Hittites before you."[5] (Ex. 23:20–23a, 27–28)

While pillars of cloud and fire had led and protected the Israelites in the past, an angel would personify the presence of Yahweh in the future. To rebel against him, become embittered, ignore, resent, or stray from this guardian would be the same as defying the living God. It would also invoke His punishment. In addition to this warning, the Israelites also learned that the Promised Land would not be theirs without a fight. For the first time, they realized that they would be intruders, conquerors, and aliens in this strange, new land. But if they trusted God completely, the battle was already won.

"But You Must . . ."

Like the promise to be God's special treasure and holy, priestly kingdom, the promise of a land of their own came with conditions:

> "You shall not worship their gods, nor serve them, nor do according to their deeds; but you shall utterly overthrow them and break their sacred pillars in pieces. But you shall serve the Lord your God, and He will bless . . . . You shall make no covenant with them or with their gods. They shall not live in your land, because they will make you sin against Me; for if you serve their gods, it will surely be a snare to you." (Ex. 23:24–25a, 32–33)

"I want you to be distinctly Mine," the Lord told them. He didn't

---

5. Notice how many promises the Lord makes to His people in His "I will" statements. He will (1) be an enemy to their enemies (v. 22), (2) destroy the pagan nations occupying the land destined for Israel (v. 23), (3) provide abundant food and water (v. 25a), (4) remove sickness (v. 25b), (5) give long life and prevent premature death, helping the population to grow (v. 26), (6) terrify Israel's enemies in advance (v. 27), (7) make Israel's enemies retreat (v. 27b), (8) send hornets to drive out the nations (v. 28), (9) allow Israel protected time to grow into the land (vv. 29–30), (10) establish spacious and firm borders for them (v. 31a), and (11) give Israel power over their enemies (v. 31b).

want them degrading themselves with man-made idols, following a man-made system of religion that often involved prostitution and child sacrifice. Any way other than His way would lead to death, and Yahweh wanted life for His people. Like a faithful and loving husband, the Lord expected faithfulness and love in return.

If the Israelites would take God seriously and trust Him completely, He would give them not only life but abundant life (see vv. 25b–26)!

The choice was theirs . . . and it is ours.

Concluding Thoughts

Just as the Lord wanted the Israelites to be His "own possession" and "a kingdom of priests and a holy nation" (19:5–6), so in Christ He has called *us* to be "a royal priesthood, a holy nation, a people for God's own possession" (1 Pet. 2:9a). Why?

> So that [we] may proclaim the excellencies of Him who has called [us] out of darkness into His marvelous light. (v. 9b)

How do we proclaim the Lord's "excellencies"? Like the Israelites did—by obeying His commands:

> "A new commandment I give to you, that you love one another, even as I have loved you, that you also love one another. By this all men will know that you are My disciples, if you have love for one another." (John 13:34–35)

> "Teacher, which is the great commandment in the Law?" And He said to him, "'You shall love the Lord your God with all your heart, and with all your soul, and with all your mind.' This is the great and foremost commandment. The second is like it, 'You shall love your neighbor as yourself.' On these two commandments depend the whole Law and the Prophets." (Matt. 22:36–40)

> Love does no wrong to a neighbor; therefore love is the fulfillment of the law. (Rom. 13:10)

When we look back to Mount Sinai, we see there a ragamuffin multitude with calloused hands and swollen feet. Their hearts heavy with anticipation and their minds unsure of the future, they covenanted with the Lord to become a new people boldly following a new purpose.

We're not so different, are we? We don't know what the future holds, but we know who holds it. And we know who holds us. May we find our hearts beating with a passion to be holy people who seek to live lives consecrated to God. May we live out the purpose He has created for us—to be lights of His love in a darkened world.

 Living Insights

As a new people, Israel was entrusted by God with a purpose to proclaim to the world: "Worship Yahweh only!" Their mission would not be easy to fulfill. Surrounded by hostile nations, the Israelites often chose to join and blend in with the world rather than to hold high God's unique calling and His light (see the book of Judges).

Christians, too, are alien people in a hostile world. We're often met with antagonism, or at the least, cynical indifference. Unlike Israel, though, we don't go to war against our critics. Instead of swords, we carry Scripture. Instead of battle cries, we proclaim love. Instead of freedom from shackles, we have been freed from sin. And instead of hailing military victories, we should be stunning the world with tangible compassion.

The Israelites had a choice: take the Lord's commands seriously and march confidently into the land, or pitch their tents forever as wanderers in the wilderness. They could trust God to provide for and protect them amidst hostility, or they could return to Pharaoh's familiar slavery.

We have a choice too: wander on this temporal planet or worship the eternal God; trust in Yahweh or trust in the world.

Do you feel more like an alien in this world or a permanent resident? Why?

_____

_____

_____

_____

_____

What does taking seriously God's commands look like in a hostile or indifferent world?

_____

_____

_____

_____

_____

_____

How are you doing at keeping Christ's new commandment to love one another (John 13:34–35)? Are you engaging the world with acts of God's compassion as vigorously as the Israelites were engaging it with acts of God's power? What are some specific ways you can carry Christ's love into your day-to-day world?

_____

_____

_____

_____

_____

_____

✝ *Invitation to Worship*

In our frenzied world of cell phones and palm pilots, soccer games and play groups, PTA and Sunday school board meetings, do we truly take time to acknowledge God's provision and protection in our lives?

We so often wander through life worrying more about the price of gasoline than appreciating Yahweh's bountiful love. By doing this, we reduce Christianity to an item on our checklist. Check off the devotion, check off the prayer, check off the Sunday service. We want God to help us influence our neighbors, raise our children, and unleash His Light in the world. But all too frequently, we expect Him to squeeze into our schedule—and please, make it quick!

Take time right now to thank God for His provision and protection in your life. Use the lines that follow to write down how He has provided for you in times of need. Recount how He has been your banner of protection in times of crisis, depression, or injustice. Reflect on how He granted you peace when all you experienced was pain. And remember how He healed you or a loved one or comforted you when you lost someone dear to your heart.

_____

_____

_____

_____

_____

_____

_____

_____

_____

_____

_____

_____

Chapter 4

GENEROSITY: WILLING HEARTS, STIRRED WITHIN

Selections from Exodus 25–36

H ow would you respond to a God whose lightest touch nearly shook a mountain off its foundation, hurtled plumes of thick smoke skyward, and tore the heavens with lightning? Whose approach was heralded by a ram's horn with a seemingly endless blast that crescendoed to an ear-splitting volume? Whose very voice rolled and crashed and thundered until your bones rattled?

Most likely, you'd do what the Israelites did: back off, knees knocking, and beg Moses to speak instead of that frightening, awesome Yahweh (Ex. 20:18–19)! Terrified, the people could only watch Moses hike up that mountain and disappear into the cloud of the Lord's presence.

When Moses came back down to present the terms of Yahweh's covenant, who wouldn't have said, "All that the Lord has spoken we will do, and we will be obedient!" (24:7; see also v. 3).

Today, we often don't sense the magnificence — and danger — of the Lord's presence. We tend to take Him for granted, treating Him casually like a buddy-God. But He's so much more. This and other scenes from Exodus can open our eyes to see Him as He is:

> Yahweh's presentation of his Presence to Israel while the nation was gathered on the plain before Horeb/Sinai is the very center of the sequence of story of the book of Exodus. In a way, it is the center also of the sequence of story of the Old Testament, and of the Bible, taken as a whole, for the coming of God is *the* subject of the biblical story.[1]

Yahweh is present with us today—what should we do? He tells us Himself: reflect His holiness in our lives (Ex. 20–23, the Law) and honor His holiness in worship (Ex. 25–31, the tabernacle).

1. John I. Durham, *Understanding the Basic Themes of Exodus* (Dallas, Tex.: Word Publishing, 1990), p. 56.

After confirming the covenant of the Law (24:3–8), the Israelites watched Moses go up the mountain of the Lord once more. This time, he received Yahweh's instructions on how to worship the Lord who wanted to live not at a distance, but close and present in their midst.

Instructions for the Tabernacle

Scholar T. Desmond Alexander tells us,

> The building of the tabernacle forms a natural sequel to the making of the divine covenant. Built according to divine instruction, the tabernacle became the focal point of the Lord's presence in the midst of the people, and reminded them, through its materials and structure, of God's sovereign, holy nature.[2]

The ways the Lord sought to involve His people in this sacred project reveal a great deal about Him and about the values He desires to see in us.

A Clear Directive

> Then the Lord spoke to Moses, saying, "Tell the sons of Israel to raise a contribution for Me; from every man whose heart moves him you shall raise My contribution." (25:1–2)

Notice, the Lord did not demand a tithe or a tax;[3] He asked for a freewill offering. The Almighty God, who has the right to demand from His people both obedience and treasures, desired contribution from only those whose hearts moved them to give. He pinpointed one qualification on the part of the giver—that his or her whole heart, or being, drive the decision.[4]

---

2. T. Desmond Alexander, "Exodus," *New Bible Commentary: 21st Century Edition*, 4th ed., rev., ed. D. A. Carson and others (Downers Grove, Ill.: InterVarsity Press, 1994), p. 93.

3. God, as sovereign King, has the right to demand anything He wants. Later in this meeting on the mountain, He instituted a temple tax of half a shekel from every person (Ex. 30:11–15). Then in Leviticus 27:30, the Lord decreed a tithe of the land and its produce.

4. For the Israelites, *heart* (*leb*) served as the center of a person's life, referring "either to the inner or immaterial nature in general or to . . . emotion, thought, or will." R. Laird Harris, Gleason L. Archer Jr., and Bruce K. Waltke, eds., *Theological Wordbook of the Old Testament* (Chicago, Ill.: Moody Press, 1980), vol. 1, p. 466.

A Specific Call

The Lord next told Moses what materials He wanted the people to contribute:

> "This is the contribution which you are to raise from them: gold, silver and bronze, blue, purple and scarlet material, fine linen, goat hair, rams' skins dyed red, porpoise skins,[5] acacia wood, oil for lighting, spices for the anointing oil and for the fragrant incense, onyx stones and setting stones for the ephod and for the breastpiece." (Ex. 25:3–7)

Only the finest things will do for the Lord Most High! John Durham notes, "The materials themselves represent a catalog of opulence: the finest metals, the finest fabrics, the finest leathers, the finest wood, the finest oil and incense and semiprecious stones."[6] As the Egyptians once plundered the Hebrews, enslaving them to make themselves wealthy, so the Israelites plundered the Egyptians at the Exodus (see Ex. 3:21–22; 12:35–36). But the Israelites didn't receive these luxuries to lavish on themselves— they gave them to the Lord.

A Stated Objective

What is the purpose of this project? The Lord Himself explained it to Moses:

> "Let them construct a sanctuary for Me, that I may dwell among them." (25:8)

Yahweh, who split the sea and shook the mountains, wanted to live with His people! The Israelites were not directed to fund a mere construction project—they were invited to participate in giving to the God of the universe. But they had to give according to Yahweh's detailed instructions:

> "According to all that I am going to show you, as

---

5. "The meaning of the Hebrew word is uncertain, and various interpretations have been offered: seal (ASV), goat (RSV), porpoise (American). A similar Arabic word means 'dolphin' or 'dugong.' Another view is that this is an Egyptian word meaning simply 'leather' (Moffatt)." Charles F. Pfeiffer and Everett F. Harrison, eds., The Wycliffe Bible Commentary (Chicago, Ill.: Moody Press, 1962), p. 74. Compare the use of the same word in Ezekiel 16:10.

6. John I. Durham, Word Biblical Commentary: Exodus (Waco, Tex.: Word Books, 1987), vol. 3, p. 354.

the pattern of the tabernacle and the pattern of all
its furniture, just so you shall construct it." (v. 9)

The Lord's sanctuary would be "a building of beauty in a barren
land and [reveal] much about the person of God and the way of
redemption."[7] The tabernacle would serve as a theological visual
aid, illustrating God's passion to be intimate with His people and
yet remain holy. So stunning, so significant, and so meaningfully
detailed would it be that those who passed by would catch their
breath and say, "The living God dwells there!"

The Lord gave detailed instructions for all of it, from the wing-
span of the cherubim on the ark of the covenant (Ex. 25:17–20)
to the number of almond blossoms on the lampstand (v. 33–34) to
the length and width of the goat-hair curtains covering the tabernacle (26:7–8). He even singled out and empowered those who
would fashion the metal, stone, and wood:

> "See, I have called by name Bezalel, the son of Uri,
> the son of Hur, of the tribe of Judah. I have filled
> him with the Spirit of God in wisdom, in under-
> standing, in knowledge, and in all kinds of crafts-
> manship, to make artistic designs for work in gold,
> in silver, and in bronze, and in the cutting of stones
> for settings, and in the carving of wood, that he may
> work in all kinds of craftsmanship. And behold, I
> Myself have appointed with him Oholiab, the son
> of Ahisamach, of the tribe of Dan; and in the hearts
> of all who are skillful I have put skill, that they may
> make all that I have commanded you." (31:2–6)

A Requirement of Rest

At the conclusion of His instructions for the tabernacle and
priestly service, the Lord reemphasized to Moses the importance of
the Sabbath:

> "As for you, speak to the sons of Israel, saying, 'You
> shall surely observe My sabbaths; for this is a sign
> between Me and you throughout your generations,
> that you may know that I am the Lord who sanctifies

---

7. Bruce Wilkinson and Kenneth Boa, *Talk Thru the Bible* (Nashville, Tenn.: Thomas Nelson
Publishers, 1983), p. 16.

you. Therefore you are to observe the sabbath, for it is holy to you. Everyone who profanes it shall surely be put to death; for whoever does any work on it, that person shall be cut off from among his people. For six days work may be done, but on the seventh day there is a sabbath of complete rest, holy to the Lord; whoever does any work on the sabbath day shall surely be put to death. So the sons of Israel shall observe the sabbath, to celebrate the sabbath throughout their generations as a perpetual covenant.' It is a sign between Me and the sons of Israel forever; for in six days the Lord made heaven and earth, but on the seventh day He ceased from labor, and was refreshed." (vv. 13–17)

The Sabbath was extremely important to the Lord, but why? From this passage we can see several reasons. First, the Sabbath was "the actual sign of the covenant."[8] It showed that the Israelites were distinct from other nations, that their lives were centered on their unique relationship with Yahweh. Second, it reminded them that it was not their work that sanctified them but the One who set them apart to be His holy people. Third, the Lord designated this day as holy, which is why anyone who disregarded it was actually disregarding their precious covenant relationship with Yahweh. They would be putting their will over His, desecrating what was holy to Him. Fourth, they were to follow the Lord's own pattern of work and rest, as a witness "to God's rule over his creation."[9]

In essence, Yahweh commanded His people to cease from their own activities and personal responsibilities in order to make time to ponder His activities, His person, His ways, His calling. Theirs was to be a lifestyle of worship.

Broken Faith and the Lord's Forgiveness

For forty days and forty nights, Moses was in the Lord's presence on Mount Sinai, faithfully writing down all of the Lord's instructions (24:18). The people, however, grew impatient; their anxiety

---

8. Brevard S. Childs, *The Book of Exodus: A Critical, Theological Commentary*, The Old Testament Library Series (Philadelphia, Pa.: Westminster Press, 1974), p. 541.

9. Childs, *The Book of Exodus*, p. 542.

over Moses' absence and their lack of control over their situation caused them to renege on the covenant with Yahweh they had so eagerly made just over a month ago:

> Now when the people saw that Moses delayed to come down from the mountain, the people assembled about Aaron and said to him, "Come, make us a god who will go before us; as for this Moses, the man who brought us up from the land of Egypt, we do not know what has become of him." (32:1)

Unbelievable, isn't it? But worse, Aaron complied. He asked for their gold (ironically, the first thing the Lord wanted them to contribute to Him [25:3]) and fashioned a golden calf, proclaiming: "This is your god, O Israel, who brought you up from the land of Egypt" (32:2–4). On the altar Aaron built, the people sacrificed burnt offerings and held a raucous feast. Ultimately, they incurred the wrath of the one true God (vv. 7–14).

Quickly, Moses descended from Mount Sinai with the two tablets of the covenant, engraved by God's own hand (vv. 15–16). When he saw the idol in the camp and the people dancing around it, he threw down the tablets in anger, shattering them—a vivid demonstration of the brokenness of the covenant (v. 19). About three thousand of the out-of-control idolaters were killed by faithful Levite priests (vv. 27–28). Suddenly sobered, the people mourned because of the Lord's threat to remove His presence from them (33:3–4).

What is even more amazing than the people's abandonment of God is God's faithfulness. He chose to remain with them. In response to Moses' intercession on behalf of the people, the Lord reassured him, "My presence shall go with you, and I will give you rest" (v. 14).

The Lord then replaced the tablets of the covenant (34:1–28), and revealed to Moses a glimpse of His character:

> "The Lord, the Lord God, compassionate and gracious, slow to anger, and abounding in lovingkindness and truth; who keeps lovingkindness for thousands, who forgives iniquity, transgression and sin; yet He will by no means leave the guilty unpunished, visiting the iniquity of fathers on the children and on the grandchildren to the third and fourth generations." (34:6–7)

Compassionate and righteous, forgiving and just—this is the Lord who renewed His covenant even with covenant-breakers (vv. 10–27). Brevard Childs offers this insightful reflection on these scenes:

> The Old Testament understood this episode of flagrant disobedience, not as an accidental straying, but as representative in its character. The story of the divine redemption includes the history of human resistance and rebellion. . . .
>
> . . . The story of the golden calf has found a place in scripture as a testimony to God's forgiveness. Israel and the church have their existence because God picked up the pieces. There was no golden period of unblemished saintliness. Rather, the people of God are from the outset the forgiven and restored community. There is a covenant—and a new covenant—because it was maintained from God's side. . . . The foundation of the covenant was, above all, divine mercy and forgiveness.[10]

The People's Response

Moses, whose face was shining from being in the presence of the Lord's glory, took the covenant and the tabernacle instructions to the forgiven and restored people (34:29–35:19).

Significantly, Moses began where the Lord ended—with the Sabbath (35:1–3). Everything the Israelites were instructed to do was based on the reality that they were to be set apart to the Lord, a people of blessing and promise and covenant. Second, Moses conveyed the Lord's direction that "whoever is of a willing heart" was to make a contribution to the Lord of all the finest materials they had (vv. 4–9). Third, Moses directed those the Lord had made skillful to fashion the tabernacle and all its furnishings and the priestly garments (vv. 10–19).

How did the people respond? With grateful, heartfelt, overwhelming generosity!

> *Everyone* whose heart stirred him and *everyone* whose spirit moved him came and brought the Lord's contribution for the work of the tent of meeting and

10. Childs, *The Book of Exodus*, pp. 579–80.

38

for all its service and for the holy garments. Then *all* whose hearts moved them, both men and women, came and brought brooches and earrings and signet rings and bracelets, all articles of gold; so did *every man* who presented an offering of gold to the Lord. *Every man*, who had in his possession blue and purple and scarlet material and fine linen and goats' hair and rams' skins dyed red and porpoise skins, brought them. *Everyone* who could make a contribution of silver and bronze brought the Lord's contribution; and *every man* who had in his possession acacia wood for any work of the service brought it. *All the skilled women* spun with their hands, and brought what they had spun, in blue and purple and scarlet material and in fine linen. *All the women* whose heart stirred with a skill spun the goats' hair. *The rulers* brought the onyx stones and the stones for setting for the ephod and for the breastpiece; and the spice and the oil for the light and for the anointing oil and for the fragrant incense. *The Israelites, all the men and women*, whose heart moved them to bring material for all the work, which the Lord had commanded through Moses to be done, brought a free-will offering to the Lord. (34:21–29, emphasis added)

Day after day, every morning, the people brought their contributions to Moses (36:3), until the workers finally told him: "The people are bringing *much more than enough* for the construction work which the Lord commanded us to perform" (v. 5, emphasis added). Moses had to order them to stop (v. 6)!

Having more than enough materials, the people proceeded to carefully carry out the Lord's directions, preparing a dwelling place for His presence (36:8–39:43).

A Concluding Thought

"From every man whose heart moves him you shall raise My contribution," the Lord told Moses (25:2). Moses told the people, "Take from among you a contribution to the Lord; whoever is of a willing heart, let him bring it as the Lord's contribution" (35:5). The people's hearts were stirred—they freely and generously lavished their finest possessions on the Lord for His tabernacle (vv. 21–29).

More than the gold, silver, bronze, fine linens, and precious stones, the Lord desires willing hearts. He chooses a love relationship with us—we are His beloved children, even His bride (see Eph. 5:1; 1 John 3:2; Isa. 54:5, Eph. 5:25–32; Rev. 19:7). The Israelites experienced this love through the Lord's miraculous deliverance of them from Egypt and through His desire to make them His unique possession among the nations. This love was brought home to them in a powerful way when the Lord forgave them, renewed His covenant with them, and restored His presence to them.

In the New Testament, we find a similar example of God's love. While Jesus was dining with a Pharisee, an immoral woman washed His feet with her tears, wiped them with her hair, and anointed them lavishly with costly perfume. The Pharisee was aghast that Jesus would allow such a woman to touch Him. But He forgave the woman her sins and explained to the Pharisee: "For this reason I say to you, her sins, which are many, have been forgiven, for she loved much; but he who is forgiven little, loves little" (Luke 7:47).

The Lord, our Lord, is

> —a God compassionate and favorably disposed;
> —reluctant to grow angry,
>   and full of unchanging love and reliableness;
> —keeping unchanging love for the thousands;
> —taking away guilt and transgression and sin.
> (Ex. 34:6–7)[11]

Let's set aside a Sabbath-time to reflect on the Lord's compassion, love, and forgiveness so that our hearts will be stirred to a deeper love and a more generous life lived for Him.

 Living Insights

You may have memorized John 1:14a: "And the Word became flesh, and dwelt among us." But did you realize that the word *dwelt* could be substituted with *tabernacled*: "And the Word became flesh and *tabernacled* among us"?

This isn't a word we use much today, yet the ancient Israelites would have appreciated the image it carries. The tabernacle served

---

11. Durham, *Understanding the Basic Themes of Exodus*, p. 76.

as a living picture of God's passion to be intimate with His people. Yahweh said to the wandering Israelites, "I want to come with you!"

Other religions in this world find human beings trying to reach up to a god, to somehow appease and manipulate a transcendent and invisible entity. But the Lord of the Bible reaches down, or condescends, to humanity. The transcendent becomes immanent. The holy dwells among the unholy.

Just as God longed to dwell among the ancient Israelites, so He longs to dwell—and reign—in the hearts of believers today. When Jesus took the form of a man, He literally "pitched His tent" alongside us. Not a moment goes by during which God does not tabernacle with His children.

So, when distance from God chokes your spirit, remember, "Be strong and courageous, do not be afraid or tremble . . . for the Lord your God is the one who goes with you. He will not fail you or forsake you" (Deut. 31:6).

 ## Invitation to Worship

Pick up your calendar, look at the week, and carve out an afternoon—or a whole day—to spend with God. Bring nothing but your Bible, your journal, a pen, and, oh yes, your checkbook. That's right. Some would say nothing is as unspiritual as money, yet Jesus affirms, "Where your treasure is, there your heart will be also" (Matt. 6:21). Worship God by asking Him to reveal the generosity of your heart through the reality of your check register.

During this time of rest and reflection, ponder the following three things about God.

His character: How has He been merciful to you? How has He been faithful to you? After a time of failure in your life, how has He shown His acceptance, compassion, and grace to you? (read John 21:15–17; Ps. 51)?

His works: How has God been generous to you? The Israelites could list specific works: the Exodus, the parting of the Red Sea, and others. What specific things can you list that God has done in your life? Write them down and let them serve as examples of God's faithfulness.

_____

_____

_____

_____

_____

His promises: Claim some promises of God's provision for your soul, your future, and your material needs. Read Matthew 6, noting especially verses 19–34.

_____

_____

_____

_____

_____

Now, look at your checkbook. Have you exemplified a life of generosity? Maybe it hasn't been with money but with acts of service, like the skilled workers we studied in this chapter. In light of God's character, His works, and His promises, has your heart been moved to respond to God specifically in the form of a freewill offering? If so, write down your commitment, and pray for personal faithfulness.

Chapter 5

INVESTING IN THINGS
ETERNAL . . . BEING BLESSED

Selections from Exodus 38–40

As we turn our eyes back to that campsite in the shadow of Sinai, we hear the clang of hammers on metal, saunter through clouds of acacia sawdust, and glide our hand across the scarlet threads woven in priestly garments. We discover a multitude of people who pledged their gifts and their skills to a massive construction project for Yahweh. They took their temporal possessions and invested in the eternal.

Did their investment pay off? What truths can we discover about sacrificing present pleasures to experience future joy?

Their Investment

The Hebrews knew exactly where their gifts and skills were going. Moses meticulously recorded how the tabernacle would be constructed, from the golden lampstands to the onyx stones in the ephod. He also kept track of the extent of their investment. He dutifully recorded all the offerings:

> All the gold that was used for the work, in all the work of the sanctuary, even the gold of the wave offering,[1] was 29 talents and 730 shekels, according to the shekel of the sanctuary. The silver of those of the congregation who were numbered was 100 talents and 1,775 shekels, according to the shekel of the sanctuary; a beka a head (that is, half a shekel according to the shekel of the sanctuary), for each one who passed over to those who were numbered, from twenty years old and upward, for 603,550 men. The hundred talents of silver were for casting the sockets of the sanctuary and the sockets of the veil; one hundred sockets for the hundred talents, a talent for a socket. Of the 1,775 shekels, he made hooks

---

1. The wave offering corresponds to the freewill offering we examined in 25:1–9 and 35:4–9.

for the pillars and overlaid their tops and made
bands for them. The bronze of the wave offering was
70 talents and 2,400 shekels. (Ex. 38:24–29)

In American currency, the amount they collected equals about
a ton of gold, close to four tons of silver, and roughly two and one-
half tons of bronze. All that from necklaces, broaches, earrings, and
captured trinkets. Imagine how much the Israelites would have
offered had Moses not heeded Bezalel's request to stop! John
Durham notes,

> The amounts of metal given in the voluntary
> offering and so recorded in the inventories are re-
> markable, and the inclusion of this information ap-
> pears to serve two purposes: (1) a further testimony
> of the joyous generosity of Israel, and (2) an addi-
> tional evidence of the magnificence of the spaces
> and the furnishings devoted to Yahweh's Presence.[2]

By today's estimates, the Israelites may have invested between
$18 million and $20 million in the tabernacle. The Israelites eagerly
and magnanimously invested in a dwelling place for the eternal God.

Their Reward

When people play the stock market or invest in real estate, the
reward is always measurable: dollars and cents dictate gain or loss.
While temporal rewards can be here today and gone tomorrow,
eternal investments yield immeasurable treasures. Let's look at three
specific rewards the Israelites received from their contributions.

Personal Accomplishment

> So the sons of Israel did all the work according to
> all that the Lord had commanded Moses. And Moses
> examined all the work and behold, they had done
> it; just as the Lord had commanded, this they had
> done. (Ex. 39:42–43a)

Look at the verbs, "Israel *did* . . . they had *done* it; just as the
Lord had commanded, this they had *done*." The Hebrews did not

---

2. John I. Durham, *Word Biblical Commentary: Exodus* (Waco, Tex.: Word Books, Publisher,
1987), vol. 3, p. 490.

just drop off their gifts and leave; they grabbed their hard hats, their hammers, and their looms. Without power tools or sewing machines, the Israelites banded together under the leadership of Bezalel and crafted by hand an elaborate sanctuary for God. They stoked the fires that melted their bracelets into gold inlay for the ark. Perhaps a mother stitched linens saved for a daughter's wedding into one of Aaron's robes.

After eleven months, they stood confidently and gratefully beside their work as Moses inspected every piece, every part, every socket that would compose this tabernacle. Solomon would later pen what they felt at that moment, "Desire realized is sweet to the soul" (Prov. 13:19a).

Personal Acknowledgment

Not only was their investment rewarded by personal accomplishment, but Moses also affirmed it:

So Moses blessed them. (Ex. 39:43b)

Moses' approval rang out over the millions arrayed before him. Eleven months prior, Moses heard the tone, the emphasis, and the precision with which God dictated His directions. In the mind of Moses, the people passed the test, and he praised them for it.

But would Yahweh approve of their work? After Moses blessed the Israelites, the Lord spoke:

"On the first day of the first month you shall set up the tabernacle of the tent of meeting. You shall place the ark of the testimony there, and you shall screen the ark with the veil." (40:2–3)

The order had been given! They passed the test. God acknowledged their work and found it satisfactory. The creation honored the Creator with the work of their hands. In the next thirteen verses, God instructed Moses to anoint every piece of the tabernacle and the priests themselves before the sanctuary was finally put together.

Then, about a year after they arrived at Mount Sinai,

in the first month of the second year, on the first day of the month, the tabernacle was erected. (v. 17)

Moses first set up the inner court, the Holy of Holies. He inserted the bars and raised the pillars; he hung the tent over the tabernacle. He placed the tablets of the Law into the ark and

45

brought along with it the sacred bread into the fifteen-foot-wide inner sanctum. He lit the lamps, placed the gold altar, and burned fragrant incense on it just as the Lord had commanded him. He hung the veil to the Holy of Holies and then went to work on the outer court. After he set up the altar of burnt offerings, Moses offered the meal offering before the Lord. He placed the laver in between the altar and the inner court. He put water into the laver, and he and Aaron and Aaron's sons purified themselves by washing their hands and feet, just as God told them to do. He put up the linen walls all around the outer court and hung the veil as the door to the outer court (see Ex. 40:1–33). "Thus Moses finished the work" (v. 33).

Personal Amazement

Then he stepped back:

> Then the cloud covered the tent of meeting, and the glory of the Lord filled the tabernacle. Moses was not able to enter the tent of meeting because the cloud had settled on it, and the glory of the Lord filled the tabernacle. (vv. 34–35)

Yahweh filled it. Just as Jesus confined Himself to a man's body and walked among us, so Almighty God confined Himself to this tent and abided with His people. The glory filled the tabernacle, and the Lord's own presence entered the Holy of Holies. Every temple the Hebrews had constructed for the countless gods of Egypt were merely empty shells compared to this. They were supposed to be the dwelling places of gods, but they were only inhabited by shadows and rodents. The One true God, however, brought His very real power and glory into the midst of His people. The house of the Lord was built; the God who was, who is, and who is to come resided on their street, in their camp.

At that moment, whatever offering the Israelites had brought, whatever gift they had sacrificed, paled in light of God's glory. On that unique day, the Israelites witnessed the magnificent, majestic, holy, almighty, self-sufficient God ablaze in the fullness of His glory.

Concluding Application

You may have a financial portfolio filled with investments that dot the spectrum from low to medium to high risk. Your emotions may rise and fall on the turbulent rides known as NASDAQ or NYSE.

Want a sure bet? Develop a spiritual portfolio—an inventory of eternal investments. Temporal gains are merely that—temporal, bound by time. Eternal investments yield eternal rewards. As the apostle Paul urged:

> Look not at the things which are seen, but at the things which are not seen; for the things which are seen are temporal, but the things which are not seen are eternal. (2 Cor. 4:18)

As the Israelites showed us, investing in the eternal brings great joy in the present—not only the joy of having completed something worthwhile, but more importantly the joy of giving something to the Lord who has given so generously to us!

> You will make known to me the path of life;
> In Your presence is fullness of joy;
> In Your right hand there are pleasures forever.
> (Ps. 16:11)

 Living Insights

Do you view gifts of charity as an opportunity for God to bless you? Or do you view giving as a duty, a salve on a guilty conscience, or as a tax write-off? Consider what Paul wrote to the Corinthians:

> Remember: A stingy planter gets a stingy crop; a lavish planter gets a lavish crop. I want each of you to take plenty of time to think it over, and make up your own mind what you will give. That will protect you against sob stories and arm-twisting. God loves it when the giver delights in the giving.
> God can pour on the blessings in astonishing ways so that you're ready for anything and everything, more than just ready to do what needs to be done.[3] (2 Cor. 9:6–8 THE MESSAGE)

You can give out of guilt, out of duty, or out of love. The God of the universe doesn't need your check. He wants to bless you

---

3. Eugene H. Peterson, *The Message: The New Testament in Contemporary English* (Colorado Springs, Colo.: NavPress, 1993), p. 380.

because of your love. Passion for God motivated the Israelites to offer their treasures. They intentionally invested in the eternal and experienced God's presence in their midst.

Is God leading you to risk the temporal for an eternal investment? Slashing part of your clothing budget could support a missionary family. Cutting down your abundant savings account could aid the church construction project. Holding off on the trampoline for the kids could benefit a local homeless shelter. Each person's finances are different, but all of us need to see what eternal investments are being or need to be made.

Pray for an opportunity to give sacrificially to an eternal investment. Write down what the Lord puts on your heart.

_____

_____

_____

_____

Sow the seed: Identify resources you were planning to use temporally. Write down how you were going to use them (vacation, new clothes, etc.).

_____

_____

_____

_____

Now identify the eternal investment you are going to make.

_____

_____

_____

_____

Commit yourself to praying daily for God to use that investment.

✝ *Invitation to Worship*

Though the Lord dwelled in the tabernacle, only the High Priest, once a year, was able to enter the presence of Yahweh (Lev. 16:2, 29–34). Through him, the people met God. Years later, the movable tabernacle became the permanent temple built by Solomon. Though the people could only imagine what took place behind the veil in the Holy of Holies, they corporately affirmed,

> How lovely are Your dwelling places,
> O Lord of hosts! . . .
> For a day in Your courts is better than a thousand
> outside.
> I would rather stand at the threshold of the house
> of my God
> Than dwell in the tents of wickedness. (Ps. 84:1, 10)

Today, through Christ, we can enter the Holy of Holies. God's Spirit makes His temple within us (1 Cor. 6:19). Though we have continual access to Him, all too often we seek the Lord only when we experience tradegy—the checkbook teeters in the red or our children suffer from illness.

Wouldn't you rather delight daily in the presence of the Lord? You can, and the Lord Himself will help and welcome you. To quiet your mind and center your heart, make time today to do the following:

- Set aside a block of time today to step into the Holy of Holies.

- Affirm the Lord's attributes: His holiness, His perfection, His omnipotence.

- Acknowledge personal sin: your shortcomings, your trespasses, your faults.

- Alleviate personal anxieties: your worries, your petitions, your hurts.

Remember, the Lord Himself invites you to

> draw near with confidence to the throne of grace,
> so that [you] may receive mercy and find grace to
> help in time of need. (Heb. 4:16)

Chapter 6

PRIORITY ONE: TAKING GOD VERY SERIOUSLY

Selections from Leviticus and Numbers

You won't find the word *priority* in the Bible. Search for it, and you'll discover that the word itself never appears. But the concept goes from cover to cover.

Open your Bible to the first page and immediately you see the priority: "In the beginning *God*" (Gen. 1:1, emphasis added). All life flows from Him and through Him. In the Sermon on the Mount, Jesus left no doubt as to what should be top priority in our lives: "But seek *first* His kingdom and His righteousness, and all these things will be added to you" (Matt. 6:33, emphasis added). And Paul wrote to the church in Colossae: "He [Christ] is before all things, and in Him all things hold together. . . . He is the beginning, the firstborn from the dead, so that He Himself will come to have first place in everything" (Col. 1:17–18).

In other words, if we take God seriously, He will be the first priority in our lives; everything else takes a distant second place. The Israelites learned this lesson the hard way through their experiences on Mount Sinai. They quickly discovered that they needed to adjust their priorities. Above all, they were to take Yahweh seriously.

The Way Things Used to Be

Let's travel back through time to 1445 B.C., when God sat the Israelites down at the foot of Sinai. This mountain range captured none of Yellowstone's majesty or Yosemite's grandeur. Several commentators describe the landscape this way:

> This was the most desolate-looking region. . . .
> The eye sees nothing but the black gravel plain
> bordered by flat-top limestone hills of a blinding
> whiteness . . . within it (Sinai region) are endless
> expanses of undulating sand-dunes, great coastal de-
> pressions, and high jutting mountains. By far, the
> greater part of the territory is practically barren, such
> vegetation as there is, being of the typically desert

kind, meager and monotonous.[1]

In this entire bleak expanse, scraggly bushes and gnarled trees provided the only scenery. Once God had the Israelites' undivided attention, He directed their eyes to His presence in the form of a cloud by day and a column of fire by night. This exodus was no game. God had promised to make Israel's name great and, in turn, Israel had vowed to serve Yahweh only.

But there was a problem—the Hebrews were Hebrews in name only. When they first came to Egypt, they were nothing more than Jacob's family fleeing a drought. Stories about Abraham, Isaac, Jacob, and Joseph may have circulated around dinner tables at night by sagacious forefathers, but the Israelite people had no traditions and no feasts to call their own. The only remaining trace of their homeland consisted of a burial cave in a place called Machpelah (Gen. 50:13).

In four hundred years, the Israelite people had gone from being the saviors of Egypt through Joseph to becoming slaves in Egypt under Pharaoh. Egyptian culture permeated their lives. They dressed according to Egyptian standards, they spoke Egyptian, they knew all the Egyptian gods, they celebrated Egyptian holidays, and they ate Egyptian cuisine. Every piece of art or scrap of literature was distinctively Egyptian. Pharaoh was their master, and his word was their law. For generations, life for the Israelites transpired on the fertile banks of the Nile. All that existed in the minds of children who grew up there were the pagan ways of thinking and the secular ideals held by Egyptian society. Egypt was *familiar*.

A New Way of Living

In the book of Exodus, God's Law was introduced to the Israelites. Chapter 20 contains the specific commandments which Yahweh personally gave to Moses on Mount Sinai. These commandments detailed how Yahweh desired His people to live. These were not mere suggestions. Breaking them had severe consequences.

The first commandment stated simply: "You shall have no other gods before Me" (Ex. 20:3). The second was much like the first: "You shall not make for yourself an idol. . . . You shall not worship them or serve them; for I, the Lord your God, am a jealous

---

1. Beno Rothenberg, Yohanan Aharoni, and Avia Hashimshoni, *God's Wilderness: Discoveries in Sinai* (New York, N.Y.: Thomas Nelson and Sons, 1962), p. 117.

God" (vv. 4–5a). In other words, "I am your God and you are to take me very seriously. I am in first place, and there is no second place. I am priority number one."

When the Israelites later chose to worship a golden calf instead of almighty God, Yahweh would have wiped them out if not for Moses' intercession (Ex. 32).[2] One commentator notes, "The calf represented Yahweh on *their* terms. Yahweh had made clear repeatedly that he would be received and worshiped only on *his* terms."[3]

From here on, the Israelites' world was not to be seen through the lens of Egypt or the surrounding nations. Israel would not make decisions out of anxiety or desperation, but out of revelation. God instituted the Law in order to rearrange His people's priorities and transform their thinking. For their own sake, the Israelites were responsible for taking Him seriously.

As we saw earlier, though Israel left Egypt, Egypt had not left them. Soon they would be going into Canaan. These Hebrew aliens would witness new fashions, new languages, new gods, new holidays, new laws, new foods, and new memories. Instead of adopting and mixing the traditions of Egypt with the culture of Canaan, God wanted Israel to be His people—eating His feasts, practicing His customs, obeying His laws, enjoying His worship, and becoming His hope for the world. Once the tabernacle was completed, God occupied the Holy of Holies for roughly fifty days (Ex. 40:17; Num. 1:1; 10:11). Israel stowed the hammers, packed up the looms, found cushions for the ground, and God indoctrinated them on how to worship, how to live, and how to organize as a nation.

Leviticus 1–10: A New Worship

The description of the sacrificial system and the section on sexual infractions in the book of Leviticus read almost like a tabloid!

---

2. Why is it that the clearest commands are often the ones so quickly broken? Why are there so many footprints past "No Trespassing" signs? Don't eat the fruit from that tree. *Crunch.* In the same way, the Israelites constantly pushed the boundaries God established. There are four major structural sections from Exodus 20 through Numbers 10. Each section involves a rebellious act. After each infraction, God punished the Israelites severely. After Yahweh covenanted with Israel concerning the Ten Commandments, Israel promptly broke the first two by constructing a golden calf (Ex. 32). Moses washed their mouths out with a golden drink (v. 20), the Levites slew three thousand apostates that day (v. 28), and the Lord vowed to eradicate all those who bowed down to the cow (vv. 33–35). Israel realized God was not kidding about His commandments.

3. John I. Durham, "Exodus," *Word Biblical Commentary* (Waco, Tex.: Word Books, 1998), vol. 3, p. 422.

Frankly, present-day Christians often find it hard to apply Leviticus and the first part of Numbers to their lives. However, for the Hebrews—a nation without a home, a government without laws, a congregation without rules of worship, and a people without a distinctive culture—it was essential. God spared the philosophy and went straight to application. He started with how to approach Him in worship.

The descendents of Levi (one of Jacob's sons) were commissioned by God to lead the nation in worship. They were a tribe of priests, completely devoted to the shepherding and teaching of Israel. While all the tribes appreciated the book containing God's commands, the tribe of Levi memorized it backwards and forwards. It was their manual on worship. They were instructed in the *way to God* (Lev. 1–10) as well as their *walk with God* (Lev. 11–27). The first section dealt with how to worship, and the last dealt with how to live.

Yahweh meticulously instructed Moses on how to build the Tabernacle in the first ten chapters of Leviticus, then He outlined precisely how the Israelites were to worship Him. Worship involved the petitions, pleas, penitence, praises, and personal responses of finite men to their infinite God. From grain offerings to sin offerings, the Israelites were trained in how unholy creation was to approach a holy God. While other religions hypothesized and formulated their own ways of appeasing shrouded gods, the Hebrews were provided a textbook on how they could fully experience God's presence and worship Him. Long would they ponder His words:

> "'By those who come near Me *I will be treated as holy*,
> And before all the people *I will be honored*.'"
> (Lev. 10:3b, emphasis added)

Yahweh let the people know: "It's My way, not your way. I am holy, you are not. Therefore you will approach Me in the manner in which I require." The wanderers realized that, as worshipers, proper reverence was non-negotiable.[4]

---

4. This message was reinforced when the people made a dire mistake. Just as they had done with the golden calf, the sons of Aaron decided to test God. Leviticus 10:1–7 recounts the tragic story of Nadab and Abihu who desecrated the Holy of Holies with a "strange fire" (v. 1). Without any warning, Yahweh immediately consumed them with His own fire (v. 2).

Leviticus 11–27: A New Way of Life

As believers, we can worship God with our instruments, our voices, our prayers, and our sacrifices, but God also desires our very *lives* to be acts of worship. Today, as well as in ancient times, God's requirement is holiness. The word for *holy* means "set apart." As you puzzle through some of Yahweh's provisos and policies for the Hebrews' way of life, realize that His purpose was to set them apart from every other culture and nation:

> "'I am the Lord your God. You shall not do what is done in the land of Egypt where you lived, nor are you to do what is done in the land of Canaan where I am bringing you; you shall not walk in their statutes. *You are to perform My judgments and keep My statutes,* to live in accord with them; I am the Lord your God. So *you shall keep My statutes and My judgments,* by which a man may live if he does them; I am the Lord.'" (Lev. 18:2b–5, emphasis added)

Hear God's command once, and you know God is serious. Hear it in stereo, and you know God is very serious.[5] Twice in three verses, God commanded the Hebrews to follow strictly His statutes. They were not to be Egyptians; they were not to be Canaanites; they were to be children of the living God. Their lives were to reflect His glory. They were diamonds surrounded by black coal, and God prepared them to sparkle with His grace.

These laws were given because Yahweh is God and the Israelites belonged to Him as a "peculiar people" (Deut. 26:18 KJV), distinctive and set apart for His glory. Next time you read Leviticus, follow each command with these words: ". . . because I want to set you apart."

Numbers 1–10: A New Organization

Finally, God concluded fifty days of commands with instructions on how the Israelites were to conquer their Promised Land. Rather than commanding armies using the conventional wisdom of the day, God had His own battle plan. Even in military organization,

---

5. Leviticus 24:10–16 tells of the trial and public execution of the son of a mixed marriage (Israelite/Egyptian) who blasphemed the name of God. This served as a deadly reminder of the dire consequences of transgressing God's Word.

the Israelites were to be distinctive and set apart. According to the book of Numbers, God grouped His army by family around the tabernacle:

> "Take a census of all the congregation of the sons of Israel, by their families, by their fathers' households, according to the number of names, every male, head by head from twenty years old and upward, whoever is able to go out to war in Israel, you and Aaron shall number them by their armies." (Num. 1:2–3)

The head of each tribe stepped up to lead his division. Elizur stood in front of Reuben's descendants, Shelumiel in front of Simeon's, Nahshon in front of Judah's, and so on down the list (Num. 1:5–16).

The Israelites would not conquer Canaan in the same manner as any other nation. Rather, they would do it as a nation of families. Standing at attention, banners unfurled, a mob was transformed into an army, sons marching side by side with fathers. With God as priority number one, Israel was ready to vanquish her foes and capture her long-awaited land.

Five Signs of People Who Take God Seriously

The nation of Israel learned that taking God seriously required lifestyle changes. In the same way, our lives look drastically different when we make the Lord our first priority.

1. *God occupies the first place, not any other place.* That means you may have to raise your children differently than your neighbors do. That means in your business you choose to value the book of Proverbs over the wisdom of Wall Street. God takes priority number one when you write your checks, when you deal with your spouse, and even in your thought life.

2. *His Word is the final word, not just another opinion.* That means we don't conform Scripture to our feelings, our philosophy, or our opinions. Scripture conforms us. That is why it's crucial to be involved enthusiastically in a local church that is committed to the authority of God's Word.

3. *Our worship is deep and meaningful, never superficial.* Worship is a response of God's people reflecting on God's grace. In a time when many churches seek to entertain crowds rather than

engage worshipers of the living God, we should strive to deepen our response and gratitude to the Lord.

4. *The values we embrace transcend culture, rather than being based upon it.* In light of our fast-paced and ever-changing culture, our values have shifted from absolutes to relativism. Still, people crave values that are stable, consistent, authentic, and relevant. Scripture provides a compass for life. This was true for Moses, and it's applicable today.

5. *The integrity of the family is protected, not compromised.* Vermont granted marital privileges to homosexuals, and many states are scrambling to ratify an amendment defining the word *family*. One day *alternative lifestyle* may mean "heterosexual, monogamous, committed-for-life." Would you be willing to be "old-fashioned and outdated" in a modern society? The church must uphold the sanctity and honor of the family.

 Living Insights

In the bustling seaport of Ephesus a vibrant church with a storied history sat on the verge of divine destruction. Years before, Paul birthed and nurtured the early church to serve as an evangelical base for all of Asia Minor. He commissioned Aquila and Priscilla to act as *de facto* parents to the church while Paul journeyed around the Mediterranean.

Paul probably penned four or five epistles during his many stays in Ephesus. Eventually, he passed the torch and allowed his protégé, Timothy, to pastor the growing congregation (1 Tim. 1:3). The beloved apostle, John, also called Ephesus home before he was exiled to the island of Patmos.

This influential church endured countless persecutions from Roman emperors, internal deception from false teachers, and membership losses from martyrdom. As its reputation heightened during the end of the first century, God questioned its passion: "But I have this against you, that you have left your first love" (Rev. 2:4). Good deeds abounded, saints persevered, and the congregation grew, but the passion that once defined the people now waned. Unless the church in Ephesus repented, the Lord threatened to "remove [its] lampstand" (Rev. 2:5). The congregation had replaced God with a mistress, and He was jealous for their passionate love.

Psychologists refer to the "seven-year itch" as a time when a husband and wife question their love for each other and the vitality of their marriage. Cobwebs cover their marriage vows. As a result, often divorce claims the marriage or the marriage succumbs to a manageable apathy. The husband or wife or both have left their first love. The couple must recommit to expressing their undying love and devotion to one another, or the marriage will inevitably crash on the shores of statistics.

In what areas have you "left your first love"? Maybe prayer once served as a fervent companion and now it only accompanies you before meals. Maybe your Bible collects more dust than fingerprints. Maybe the desire to impact people for Christ has been replaced by the desire to increase profits. God is jealous for your passion. It's time to get serious with Him again.

Are there areas that you have been prioritizing above your relationship with God? If so, list them here:

_____

_____

_____

_____

_____

_____

Write down how you will return to your first love and once again get serious with God. For accountability purposes, you may want to share your confession with a trusted friend. Make a serious commitment and a realistic plan, and stick to it!

_____

_____

_____

_____

_____

_____

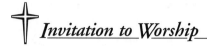

Invitation to Worship

The Westminster Confession states: "The chief end of man is to glorify God and enjoy Him forever." John Piper tweaks this statement in his book *Desiring God* by declaring: "The chief end of man is to glorify God *by* enjoying him forever."[6] As believers, we have been created to enjoy and celebrate the presence of God.

In a land stripped of vegetation, scenery, and distractions, the budding nation of Israel reveled in the presence of God. When was the last time we reveled in anything other than a medium designed for our senses? Our culture bombards us with sensual entertainment and the lure of escape. So many things vie for our attention. Evenings rarely exist without television. Radios blare at us as we turn the key in the ignition. Noise feels normal and silence uncomfortable.

Think about the last time you *enjoyed* the presence of God. Too often, we treat our quiet times as tasks to check off our to-do list rather than as meetings with an eternally gratifying God. C. S. Lewis stated that the problem with our culture is that "we are far too easily pleased."[7] The opportunity for eternal fulfillment rests on our doorstep, but so often we trade it in for fleeting and ultimately unfulfilling diversions.

Jesus made it a practice to periodically retreat to the mountains to worship His Father. Find a retreat for yourself—a place away from the lights, the cell phone, the distractions, and the demands of daily life. Take a sabbatical from the noise, escape from entertainment, and allow yourself to enjoy the presence of God. Bring some of your favorite psalms and recite them back to God. Invite God to inhabit your praises to Him. Read 1 Chronicles 16:8–36 and sing with David:

> Ascribe to the Lord,
> O families of the peoples,
> Ascribe to the Lord glory and strength.
> Ascribe to the Lord the glory due His name;
> Bring an offering, and come before Him;
> Worship the Lord in holy array. (vv. 28–29)

6. John Piper, *Desiring God* (Portland, Ore.: Multnomah Press, 1986), p. 14.

7. C. S. Lewis, "The Weight of Glory," quoted in Piper, *Desiring God,* p. 16.

As you experience His presence, chronicle your enjoyment of Him:

_____

_____

_____

_____

_____

_____

_____

_____

_____

_____

_____

_____

Chapter 7

IT'S TIME TO CELEBRATE—
NOT COMPLAIN

Numbers 10:11–17; 11:1–6; 12:1–4, 9–10

The world is full of complainers, isn't it? Unions voice the complaints of employees. Lobbyists stress their partisan pleas in the halls of Congress. Comment cards at restaurants have a designated spot for "things we can do better." Husbands gripe about nagging wives, and wives murmur to friends about their passive husbands. And what about kids? Sure, yours may seem like little angels . . . until you put broccoli on their plates!

But at least the body of Christ models people living in harmony, right? Not always! Chuck Colson states in his book *The Body:*

> It is not difficult to understand the two most frequent reasons people give for avoiding church: "All Christians are hypocrites," and "Christians are always fighting with each other."
>
> To the first I invariably reply, "Sure, probably so. Come on and join us. You'll feel right at home." But I haven't come up with a very good answer to the second.[1]

Unfortunately, many churches are characterized by divisions, conflicts, and complaints. Elders mumble about the pastor's personality. The pastor grumbles about the elders or deacons probing into his business. The congregation mutters about the color of the carpet. And when it comes to choosing a worship style, everyone has an opinion!

As we will soon see, after three days on the road, complaints and divisions began to characterize the Israelite people as well. Let's take a look at chapter 10 of the book of Numbers to see what caused them to lose their focus.

---

1. Charles Colson and Ellen Santilli Vaughn, *The Body* (Dallas, Tex.: Word Publishing, 1992), pp. 101–2.

Pack 'Em Up and Move 'Em Out!

> Now in the second year, in the second month, on
> the twentieth of the month, the cloud was lifted
> from over the tabernacle of the testimony; and the
> sons of Israel set out on their journeys from the
> wilderness of Sinai. (Num. 10:11–12a)

The Israelites woke up one day to find that the cloud had
moved, so they yanked up their tent pegs. Women wrapped up their
belongings while their husbands tethered the livestock. Kids scur-
ried about, eagerly anticipating their new adventure. For just under
a year, these Hebrews had camped in the shadow of Sinai. They
had listened intently to instructions on how to worship, live, and
conquer the Promised Land. Now, they were finally on the move!

Anticipation mounted as the last traces of the tent community
vanished under the dust of the Israelites' feet. Moses began his road
trip once again with nearly two million people in tow. From the
wilderness of Sinai, the people moved towards the wilderness of
Paran. These former slaves were about to become conquerors; the
wanderers were about to become worshipers. All the people had to
do was *walk:*

> Thus they set out from the mount of the Lord
> three days' journey, with the ark of the covenant of
> the Lord journeying in front of them for the three
> days, to seek out a resting place for them. The cloud
> of the Lord was over them by day when they set out
> from the camp. (Num. 10:33–34)

Are We There Yet?

All of this walking proved too much for some of the Israelite
people. Many must have thought three days was enough. Instead of
singing praises to Yahweh or snappy traveling songs to pass the time,
the people began to complain as they grew more and more weary:

> Now the people became like those who com-
> plain of adversity in the hearing of the Lord . . . .
> (Num. 11:1a)

The Hebrew word used here for *complain* means "to murmur."
Ron Allen notes that this part of the verse could be translated
literally, "Now the people became truly murmurous, an offense to

Yahweh's ears."[2] Like the dull grumbling of distant thunder, some of the Israelites began to lodge complaints against the great Yahweh.

How utterly preposterous! What "adversity" had befallen these sojourners? The Israelites had every reason to celebrate and virtually no reason to complain. Look at Yahweh's track record: with a flick of His hand, God drowned the Egyptian taskmasters under the weight of two towering walls of water. Never again would God's people labor under the crack of a whip. When hunger gnarled their stomachs, He provided bread from heaven. When throats panted for water, He cracked open a rock, and water gushed forth to quench their thirst. What more could the people want?

Furthermore, God's people were about to enter a land where hornets would sweep away their enemies (Ex. 23:28). They would live in cities they did not build, find homes they did not furnish, drink water from wells they did not dig, and eat fresh fruit from orchards they did not plant. Instead of whining, there should have been singing; instead of grumbling, there should have been dancing. Had God met every need? Yes. Was there any promise not completely fulfilled? No. But just three days into the journey, some Israelites were beginning to sound like the petulant child in the backseat asking, "Are we there yet?" So God answered them:

> When the Lord heard it, His anger was kindled, and the fire of the Lord burned among them and consumed some of the outskirts of the camp. (Num. 11:1b)

Without a word of warning, God's anger sparked into a raging fire that engulfed some of the murmurers whose tents were located around the outskirts of the camp. The column of fire that had once led the Israelites on their journey now consumed some of them. Fearing more retribution, these wayward sheep bleated in fear to their shepherd Moses:

> The people therefore cried out to Moses, and Moses prayed to the Lord and the fire died out. So the name of that place was called Taberah, because the fire of the Lord burned among them. (Num. 11:2–3)

---

2. Ronald Allen, "Numbers," *The Expositor's Bible Commentary*, ed. Frank Gaebelein (Grand Rapids, Mich.: Zondervan Publishing House, 1990), vol. 2, p. 786.

Moses quickly responded with a desperate prayer—a plea to spare them from total destruction. The word for "prayer" here was often used when a petitioner was seeking to avert God's wrath (compare Gen 20:7, 17; Deut 9:20, 26).[3] The name *Taberah* literally means "burning." This sobering event served as a deadly reminder of the consequences that the people would face when they chose to test God rather than trust Him (Deut. 9:22).

Desiring Cucumbers More than the Creator

Those who complained revealed their lack of trust. Can you imagine grumbling after viewing a public execution for the same offense? The Israelites acted foolishly by continuing to mutter against God, believing that qualifying their complaints would somehow appease Him. It's clear that the main source of their chagrin was their stomachs:

> "We remember the fish which we used to eat free in Egypt, the cucumbers and the melons and the leeks and the onions and the garlic, but now our appetite is gone. There is nothing at all to look at except this manna." (Num. 11:5–6)

Note that the Israelites weren't complaining about the lack of food. They had plenty . . . of manna! They were complaining about the lack of variety in their meals. Numbers describes the staple of their diet this way:

> Now the manna was like coriander seed, and its appearance like that of bdellium. The people would go about and gather it and grind it between two millstones or beat it in the mortar, and boil it in the pot and make cakes with it; and its taste was as the taste of cakes baked with oil. (Num. 11:7–9)

Sound tasty? After almost a year of going through "1,001 Ways to Cook Manna," they believed they had a right to lodge their complaints. They desired rich food, pleasant food. Specifically, they desired *Egyptian* food.

The Hebrews were obsessing over certain things they had in

---

3. Philip J. Budd, "Numbers," *Word Biblical Commentary* (Waco, Tex.: Word Books, 1984), vol. 5, p. 120.

Egypt. "Eat free" in verse 5 was an ironic statement. They should have said, "Eat freely as slaves." They remembered the culinary delights, but conveniently forgot the whips. These emancipated Israelites were ready to trade in their freedom for slavery. They were ready to swap the Creator for cucumbers. They focused on lack rather than abundance. Rather than celebrating Yahweh's provision, they criticized it.

Moses Questions His Calling

The complainers built momentum because the people began to believe God's antagonists rather than God's anointed. As seen above, the Lord's shocking punishment did not deter the antagonists. Instead, the whining and grumbling began to affect the whole community and prompted their leader to question his calling:

> So Moses said to the Lord, "Why have You been so hard on Your servant? And why have I not found favor in Your sight, that You have laid the burden of all this people on me? . . . I alone am not able to carry all this people, because it is too burdensome for me. So if You are going to deal thus with me, please kill me at once, if I have found favor in Your sight, and do not let me see my wretchedness." (Num. 11:11, 14–15)

After God relayed His displeasure, Moses revealed his despondency. He basically said to God, "Remember what I told You when You first appeared to me in the burning bush? I'm not qualified to lead these people. I'm not the right man for this job!"

Practical Advice and a Spiritual Rebuke

Yahweh dealt with the desperation of Moses, as well as the discomfort of the grumblers. He gave Moses some very practical help to keep him from being overburdened with the task of leading the people. And He showed him how to avoid micromanagement:

> The Lord therefore said to Moses, "Gather for Me seventy men from the elders of Israel, whom you know to be the elders of the people. . . . I will take of the Spirit who is upon you, and will put Him upon them; and they shall bear the burden of the

people with you, so that you will not bear it all alone." (Num. 11:16–17)

As for the discomfort of the carnivorous grumblers, Yahweh responded in a way that calls to mind the words of a wise man: "Be careful what you wish for. You just might get it!" God said,

> "You shall eat, not one day, nor two days, nor five days, nor ten days, nor twenty days, but a whole month, until it comes out of your nostrils and becomes loathsome to you; because you have rejected the Lord who is among you and have wept before Him, saying, 'Why did we ever leave Egypt?'"
> (Num. 11:19–20)

Talk about an all-protein diet! Moses, already exasperated, responded much like twelve men would do later when Jesus asked them to feed five thousand people with a boy's sack lunch.

> "Should flocks and herds be slaughtered for them, to be sufficient for them? Or should all the fish of the sea be gathered together for them, to be sufficient for them?" (Num. 11:22)

Moses frantically looked for a practical solution to a supernatural problem. He quickly counted up all the livestock. "No, not enough. And even if there were a sea in the middle of the desert, you could fish it dry and serve only appetizers." God deftly rebuked Moses in the form of a question.

> The Lord said to Moses, "Is the Lord's power limited? Now you shall see whether My word will come true for you or not." (v. 23)

The literal rendering of this phrase is, "Is the Lord's arm too short?" God asks this rhetorical question in reference to Himself. In other words, "What's the matter? Is my arm too short to reach all the way down to you and help you? Have I ever left you high and dry before?"

Yahweh reminded Moses: "Remember who you are dealing with, Moses! Don't you remember the plagues? What about the parting of the Red Sea and the last time I provided a quail feast (see Ex. 16:8–13)? Can you name even one time when My power was not enough?" The answer, of course, was no. Moses couldn't.

Just Desserts

The Creator and Commander of the universe ordered the wind to bring flocks of quail to the Israelites. Birds appeared as far as the eye could see, "about a day's journey on this side and a day's journey on the other side" (Num. 11:31). Feathers flew as fowl piled up about three feet deep. It took two days to gather them all, and even the most challenged bird-catcher managed to gather almost sixty bushels of quail. Ron Allen sums up the scene in a unique way:

> The scene must have been similar to a riot: people screaming, birds flapping their wings, everywhere the pell-mell movement of a meat-hungry people in a sea of birds. Dare we picture people ripping at the birds, eating flesh before cooking it, bestial in behavior? They must have been like a sugar-crazed boy in a child's daydream, afloat on a chocolate sandwich cookie raft in a sea of chocolate syrup, nibbling at the cookie before drowning in the dark, sweet sea.[4]

In their excitement, the people reveled in the gift but forgot the Giver. And guess what happened just as the meat touched their lips:

> While the meat was still between their teeth, before it was chewed, the anger of the Lord was kindled against the people, and the Lord struck the people with a very severe plague. So the name of that place was called Kibroth-hattaavah. (Num. 11:33–34a)

Kibroth-hattaavah means "graves of craving." What a picture! These people craved flesh over faith and received their just desserts. The apostle Paul describes such revelers in Phil. 3:19 this way: "Their future is eternal destruction. Their god is their appetite, they brag about shameful things, and all they think about is this life here on earth" (NLT).

Instead of celebration, there was mourning; instead of feasting, there was weeping, and instead of dancing, a dirge. Rather than walking unhindered to Canaan, the Israelites were forced to stop and dig graves for the greedy because they had chosen to complain rather than celebrate God's gracious gifts.

---

4. Allen, "Numbers," p. 795.

Application

So, how can we apply to our own lives the lessons we've learned from the Israelites? How do we quell complaining and seek celebration? First of all, *focus on abundance rather than lack*. The people had food, but not the "right" food. In the same manner, we tend to focus on our perceived lack rather than our abundance in Christ. We have money, but not ever quite enough. We have the Palm Pilot VII, but we now need the Palm Pilot XX. We have a decent home, but it could be bigger. We live in the land of "If I only had _____, then I would be happy." We trade in God's provisions for temporal gains. We trade in our integrity for a job promotion. We trade our quality time with our spouse and kids for monetary gain. We trade in our Creator for cucumbers.

It's time for a change. It's time for us to journey with God, celebrating His provision rather than complaining about our plight. Remember the apostle Paul? He experienced severe hardship and persecution, yet he was able to sing in the depths of a Roman jail. He had learned to celebrate Yahweh despite his circumstances. Write this memorable verse from Paul on a note card and stick it in your wallet or purse, as a reminder:

> "Not that I speak from want, for I have learned to be content in whatever circumstances I am." (Phil. 4:11)

Believe in God's anointed more than God's adversaries. Leaders are constantly out in front and all too often seem to wear a target on their backs labeled, "Criticism—Take your best shot." Critics always know when things are going wrong, and rarely know when they are on the right track. God has anointed a leader in your life. It could be a pastor, a small group leader, a family member, a husband, or a boss. Write a letter of encouragement to him or her this week. Celebrate the leadership that God has provided for you.

Assume God's power even in present pain. When we cry upward and the heavens seem to respond with silence, we must realize that God has already spoken. We have hope because of what He has already done. When pain reaches its pinnacle, write down how God has delivered you in the past. If He seems to be withholding something from you, it's not because He does not have the power. Remember what He said about Himself in Numbers 11:23? His arm is not too short. His power is not limited. He desires to transform you into what you could not become on your own.

Revel in the Giver and not the gifts. If only the Israelites had been as passionate about their God as they were about having meat to eat! If only we could see how Satan, the enemy of our souls, uses superficial issues and material distractions to draw us away from our first love. Take a moment to recognize that "every good thing given and every perfect gift is from above, coming down from the Father of lights" (James 1:17a). It's time we find our contentment in our God. Our relationship with Him is the only thing that can never be taken away from us.

 Living Insights

A young boy tugged on his grandfather's tunic and asked, "Papa, why are these stones set up?" The wrinkled sage bent down and said, "Let me tell you about the deliverance of Yahweh." For each stone, he told a story. The Red Sea parted. Water gushed from a rock. Enemies were destroyed. Cities fell. Whenever circumstances threatened to overwhelm the people, Yahweh stepped in.

Joshua 4:1–14 contains God's command to His people to stack twelve stones at the Jordan to commemorate the Israelites' crossing into the Promised Land. If empires threatened Israel's borders, if locusts ravaged the crops, if Israel ever wondered whether Yahweh cared, they could go to the Jordan River. As long as they walked with the Lord, His faithfulness in the past ensured His faithfulness in the future.

Sometimes it's hard for us to remember that in the midst of cancer, God is there. Under the mounting bills, He is there. When your children turn away, He is there. Despite your husband or wife's unfaithfulness, He is there. Despite your pain, your heartache, your grief, and your loss, He wants you to take a moment to remember how He has delivered you in the past. And He will gladly do it again.

Take some time right now to chronicle God's victories in your past. Construct your own memorial—your own twelve stones which remind you of God's love, care, and provision for you throughout your life. List here the ways that God has shown His faithfulness to you.

_____

_____

_____

✝ *Invitation to Worship*

Where do you turn when you are miffed at God? What if, like the Israelite people, you are feeling frustrated about your life or your circumstances? When you hurt or are angry and you want to give God a piece of your mind, simply turn to the Psalms. This is where God's "complaint box" is found.

After studying the way the Israelites complained rather than celebrated what God had done for them, an easy conclusion to make would be that all complaining is wrong. But the Israelites complained because they *didn't believe God was sufficient*. The Psalmist knows that God has the ability to help and pleads for Him to do so. It's the difference between indignation toward God and desperation for God.

In the Psalter, we find many psalms called "laments." They usually follow this pattern: a plea to God, followed by an account of pain or a complaint, and lastly, an affirmation of God's ability to save.

Examine closely these statements from the Psalms:

> I am weary with my sighing;
> Every night I make my bed swim,
> I dissolve my couch with my tears. (6:6)

> Lord, why do you stand so far away?
> Why do you hide when I need you the most?
> (10:1 NLT)

> I am exhausted and completely crushed.
> My groans come from an anguished heart.
> (38:8 NLT)

Now, read each of the these psalms in its entirety. Do you have a reason to cry out to God? Then lift your heart to the Lord, making your needs known. Remember that God's ways are higher than ours. Ultimately, He is in control. Write out your own psalm now. Lift up your personal plea to God, give an account of your pain, and affirm His ability to save. He will give you strength and victory in His name.

Plea to God: _____

_____

_____

_____

_____

_____

Account of Pain: _____

_____

_____

_____

_____

Affirmation of Ability: _____

_____

_____

_____

_____

_____

Chapter 8

HOW TO FAIL—IN FOUR SIMPLE LESSONS

Selections from Numbers 13 and 14

An employee of the cruise line that built the *Titanic* boasted, "Not even God Himself could sink this ship."[1]

God didn't need to sink the ship; He merely allowed human arrogance to run its course. The deadly combination of unnecessary speed, little to no visibility, and pride led to the unthinkable. On its maiden voyage, the magnificent *Titanic*, steaming across the ocean with great anticipation and unlimited promise, collided with an iceberg and sank in the icy waters of the North Atlantic. The name *Titanic* is now synonymous with a tragedy of catastrophic proportions.

It had been over a year since the Israelites had fled Egypt, and now they were boarding their "dream ship." They stood on the doorstep of their destiny, embarking on their maiden voyage to freedom and seeking to find port. Forty days had passed since twelve Israelite men had sneaked into Canaan to spy out the land. Great anticipation energized the camp as the Hebrews saw the twelve spies finally return from their mission with a bunch of grapes so huge that it had to be slung across a pole and carried by two strong men! This was merely a *glimpse* of the unlimited resources and promises assured by Yahweh.

But before the wanderers could sail into the Promised Land, an iceberg of fear jutted up at Kadesh-barnea, right on the edge of Canaan.

Four Lessons in Faithlessness

As we travel back in time, we'll discover four lessons in faithlessness that led to the Israelites' utter collapse at the border of the Promised Land. Understanding these points will help us stay afloat next time we find ourselves in over our heads.

---

1. National Archives and Records Administration. Available at http://www.nara.gov/ex-hall/originals/titanic.html, accessed December 22, 2001.

Lesson One: When You Focus on the Obstacles Rather than the Objective, Fear Will Eclipse Your Faith

Laden with huge clusters of grapes, the spies reported to Moses:

> "We went in to the land where you sent us; and it certainly does flow with milk and honey, and this is its fruit." (Num. 13:27b)

That was the good news. "Yes, the milk is flowing, and the honey practically jumps right onto our biscuits, just like God said it would!" But just as Moses savored this music to his ears, these spies changed their tune:

> "Nevertheless, the people who live in the land are strong, and the cities are fortified and very large; and moreover, we saw the descendants of Anak there. Amalek is living in the land of the Negev and the Hittites and the Jebusites and the Amorites are living in the hill country, and the Canaanites are living by the sea and by the side of the Jordan." (Num. 13:28–29)

The twelve spies weren't surprised to find grapes, but they were shocked to find mighty warriors. Why were they astounded by the armies? Didn't God tell them about the milk, the honey, and the occupying forces long before, as recorded in the book of Exodus? Just as Yahweh provided the fruit, He promised to clear the land before them—with hornets, if necessary.

The great emperor and war general Napoleon Bonaparte once said, "He who fears being conquered is sure of defeat." Some of the Israelite spies were fearful of being conquered. And sure enough, you will not find Shammua, Shaphat, or Palti among the top fifty biblical names used today. You don't hear boys named Gaddi or Ammiel or Sethur replying to the roll call in first grade. However, you might see a Caleb scaling a jungle gym or a Joshua playing soccer with his friends. This is because when twelve spies scouted out the land God promised to Israel, only two faithful visionaries saw the objective as possible—Joshua and Caleb.

"We should by all means go up and take possession of it, for we will surely overcome it" boasted Caleb in Numbers 13:30. The faith of Joshua and Caleb eclipsed their fear. The other ten spies forgot the objective and saw only obstacles. They allowed their fear to eclipse their faith. Consequently, they died in obscurity somewhere in the wilderness.

The original objective was to send out twelve men, leaders of their respective tribes, to scout the land for strategy, not plausibility. The question was not *if* they could take the land, but *how* they would take it.

Read Numbers 13:17–20. You'll find no trepidation in the voice of Moses as he gave his command. But what did he receive in return? Twelve sets of eyes—and two diametrically opposed reports. Ten of the men saw seasoned armies poised for victory; Caleb saw inferior forces ready to retreat. Ten analyzed fortified cities; Joshua spied out his future home. Ten men saw Amalek, and their knees quaked; but Joshua and Caleb saw an already-vanquished foe (Ex. 17:8–16). Ten saw permanent residents, but two saw squatters on *their* property. Some believed their eyes, but Caleb and Joshua believed their ears. Yahweh had stated on at least seventeen occasions that He was going to give the land of Canaan to the sons of Israel.

Sadly, fear shipwrecked the faith of ten of Israel's tribal leaders and relegated them to a historical footnote. These men allowed the obstacles to overshadow their objectives, saying, "We are not able to go up against the people, for they are too strong for us" (Num. 13:31b). And they missed out on God's blessing due to their lack of faith. They never entered the Promised Land.

Lesson Two: When You Compare Giants to Grasshoppers, Intimidation Will Replace Confidence

With the skill of savvy orators, these ten cowards caused two million people to quiver with fear:

> So they gave out to the sons of Israel a bad report of the land which they had spied out, saying, "The land through which we have gone, in spying it out, is a land that devours its inhabitants; and all the people whom we saw in it are men of great size." (Num. 13:32)

According to their reports, the very land "devoured its inhabitants." The spies may have been referring to infertility, a dreaded problem in the ancient Near East. One commentator suggests, "It may be that the phrase is meant to denote 'destruction' generally. The land is both infertile and insecure . . . the metaphor is a way of saying that Yahweh's land is like Sheol, a devouring monster."[2] These spies exclaimed, "This land looks more like hell than heaven!"

Furthermore, the spies capitalized on another fear by mentioning the giants who lived in the land:

> "There also we saw the Nephilim (the sons of Anak are part of the Nephilim); and we became like grasshoppers in our own sight, and so we were in their sight." (Num. 13:33)

Everything seems larger when you are looking at life through fear-colored lenses. These men felt like grasshoppers compared to the huge warriors in Canaan. The only defense grasshoppers have against giants is flight, but they forgot that the greatest power and might was on their side. His name was Yahweh.

Ten spies' faith shipwrecked on the border of Canaan when they compared what they lacked with what others possessed. In the process, intimidation replaced confidence, and fear squelched faith.

Lesson Three: When You Allow Emotion to Run Rampant, Your Desire for Relief Will Weaken Your Courage

After the exaggerated and faithless report of the ten spies, panic swept through the group of sojourners like a blazing prairie fire in the middle of August. Canaan was terrifying, and in comparison Egypt seemed like heaven. The Israelites allowed their emotions to take control of their situation, as evidenced by their response to the spies' report:

> Then all the congregation lifted up their voices and cried, and the people wept that night. All the sons of Israel grumbled against Moses and Aaron; and the whole congregation said to them, "Would that we had died in the land of Egypt! Or would that we had died in this wilderness! Why is the Lord bringing us into this land, to fall by the sword? Our wives and our little ones will become plunder; would it not be better for us to return to Egypt?" So they said to one another, "Let us appoint a leader and return to Egypt." (Num. 14:1–4)

---

2. Philip J. Budd, "Numbers," *Word Biblical Commentary* (Waco, Tex.: Word Books, 1984), vol. 5, p. 145.

The people panicked. They had not experienced even one skirmish with the enemy, and yet the crowd was already predicting that the Israelite armies would be slain, their wives turned into concubines, and their little children sold into slavery.

Yahweh was less than pleased. He retorted to Moses, "How long will this people spurn Me? And how long will they not believe in Me, despite all the signs which I have performed in their midst?" (Num. 14:11) It's amazing how quickly the people's past victories vanished from their collective memory. Suddenly God's Word and His promises were put on the shelf based on a single skewed and disputed report. Preparations were even made to run back to oppressive slavery in Egypt! Ron Allen eloquently sums up the people's response:

> The more the people wailed, the more excessive their words. The more the people cried, the more they outreached one another in protests of rage. This is the crowd psychology that leads to riots, lynchings, stormings, and rampages. Now they begin to aim their anger more directly at Yahweh himself. Moses and Aaron were the fall guys, but the Lord was the one really to blame; he had delivered them from Egypt. He had brought Pharaoh to his knees . . . had led them through a barren land. . . . God was the one at fault! And they began to curse him, to condemn his goodness, to reject his grace."[3]

Their emotion, rather than God's revelation, dictated their actions.

Lesson Four: When You Desire Instant Gratification over Character Cultivation, Disaster Awaits

God had heard enough. The people were insisting on instant gratification rather than the cultivation of character. Only another selfless intervention by Moses saved these people from total and immediate annihilation by Yahweh (Num. 14:13–19). The Israelites desired instantaneous relief from their perceived plight. Rather than trusting God to protect them through the struggle, they were

---

3. Ronald Allen, "Numbers," *The Expositors Bible Commentary*, (Grand Rapids, Mich.: Zondervan Publishing House, 1990), vol. 2, p. 814.

ready to return to the familiar—even slavery in Egypt. So God caused them to wander until they perished. He would make their children conquerors, but force the complainers to become perpetual nomads:

> "'As I live,' says the Lord, 'just as you have spoken in My hearing, so I will surely do to you; your corpses will fall in this wilderness, even all your numbered men, according to your complete number from twenty years old and upward, who have grumbled against Me.'" (Num. 14:28–29)

It must have been wonderful to be nineteen, but terrible to be twenty or older!

Yahweh continued:

> "'Surely you shall not come into the land in which I swore to settle you, except Caleb the son of Je-phunneh and Joshua the son of Nun. Your children, however, whom you said would become a prey—I will bring them in, and they will know the land which you have rejected. But as for you, your corpses will fall in this wilderness. Your sons shall be shep-herds for forty years in the wilderness, and they will suffer for your unfaithfulness, until your corpses lie in the wilderness.'" (Num. 14:30–33)

This wandering in the wilderness lasted forty years—one year for every day the spies were gone (v. 34). As for the men who convinced close to two million people of their imminent demise, "those men who brought out the very bad report of the land died by a plague before the Lord" (v. 37). At the edge of their beautiful Promised Land, the Hebrews were commanded by the Lord to turn their heels, "and set out to the wilderness by the way of the Red Sea" (v. 25b). They were to return to those shores where God performed the great miracle of deliverance. From the edge of Egypt, through the wilderness, to the borders of Canaan, they were forced to wander until they died.

Instead of sailing through to Canaan, the Israelites capsized. Pride and lack of faith in Yahweh were on one side of the coin, and fear was on the other. In the tragic demise of the *Titanic*, over fifteen hundred lives were lost. But Israel's "shipwreck" sank an entire generation—over one million of God's chosen people.

Four Positive Applications for Avoiding a Shipwreck

God assures us of His unfailing love and unlimited promises when we choose to accept and follow Him. So why do we sometimes find ourselves capsizing rather than sailing to a victorious life? Our faith often shipwrecks on the shores of laziness, doubt, insecurity, fear, immorality, and apathy. But if we strive to apply the principles we have uncovered in this chapter, we will begin to overcome the fear and other obstacles that hinder our own journey toward the promised land.

First, *focus on the objective, not the obstacles.* Take a moment to read Hebrews 12:1–2. Notice the first verse: "Since we are surrounded by so great a cloud of witnesses" (NKJV). These witnesses are great men and women of the faith who refused to let obstacles, barriers, or their limited knowledge get in the way of God's objectives in their lives. The "Hall of Faith" in Hebrews 11 lists the heroes and heroines of Christianity who, despite their failings, were characterized by their vision and faith in God.

Second, *refuse to compare.* Never, ever, in any circumstance, compare what you think you lack with what others possess, especially those with great gifts. Comparison paralyzes. It prompts us to question God about our ability rather than to trust Him for the results. Our lives would change dramatically if we refused to compare our teaching skills to those of our pastors or professors, refused to compare our looks to those of the models on magazine covers, or refused to compare our church's membership with that of the church down the street. Remember, God has individually gifted you to do the work He has called you to do. We are all simply instruments in the hands of the Master Craftsman.

Third, *trust revelation over emotion.* When fog clouds the horizon and the stars are blotted from view, sailors don't put much stock in their gut feelings for direction. They trust a navigational device to guide them safely to port. When the world tells us to trust our feelings and "go with our hearts," no one takes into consideration that our hearts are ultimately self-serving. We too often make decisions based on how we feel at the time rather than on the solid principles of God's Word. We are instructed in Proverbs to trust in the Lord with all our hearts, and not to lean on our own understanding. When we choose to acknowledge Him in all our ways, He will make our paths straight (3:5–6). God's infallible Word is our compass when our emotions run rampant.

Fourth, *choose character over comfort.* God forges our character in the crucible of our trials. Because of the pain and discomfort, we are often tempted to escape back to the familiar, back to Egypt. But Yahweh wants to sculpt His image into our lives. That means we must trust God during the choppy seas of a rough marriage rather than abandon ship. That means we are called to take a stand for righteousness at our job rather than acquiesce to preserve our paycheck. Even when we can't see all that lies ahead, we must trust God's promises. After all, He is Yahweh. He always does what He says He will do.

 Living Insights

Avoiding shipwrecks does not guarantee smooth sailing. In fact, if the life of Paul is any example, once we begin that voyage of Christianity, we are probably destined to weather more storms than calm seas. Paul experienced blinded eyes, a bruised body, excommunication, abandonment, shackles, imprisonment, ridicule, scorn, and yes, even three real-life shipwrecks! Yet he lived his life in a way that honored God and deepend his faith.

Paul spoke to young Timothy of two men who crashed on a reef of spiritual failure: "Some have rejected and suffered shipwreck in regard to their faith. Among these are Hymenaeus and Alexander, whom I have handed over to Satan, so that they will be taught not to blaspheme" (1 Tim. 1:19b–20).

We all know people who might find themselves in such a letter from a modern-day Paul. In fact, on some occasions, it might be one of us. Capsized faith or shipwrecked integrity brings down more than just the individual. It affects spouses, children, parents, coworkers, the church body, and the list goes on. Are there any areas of your life in which you feel shipwrecked? Your spiritual walk? Your relationship with your parents? Your kids? Your marriage? Your friendships? Your personal life? If so, what is the situation? What does God's Word say about this issue? What can you do to change it? Where can you turn to find help and encouragement? Turn each of these areas over to God, praying that He will keep your ship afloat and clear of spiritual failure. Write your thoughts in the space provided on the next page.

_____

_____

_____

_____

_____

_____

_____

_____

_____

_____

_____

✝ _Invitation to Worship_

The winds buffeted the ship before the men actually saw the storm. Suddenly, a leisurely cruise became a fight for survival. Even seasoned fishermen cowered under the enormous waves. But a carpenter slept soundly in the hull until the disciples woke Him. Sea spray pelted His face as He said, "Why are you so timid, you men of little faith?" (Matt. 8:26)

Then Jesus spoke a word. Suddenly, the wind stopped. Instantly, the tempestuous sea became as still as glass. Immediately, the men marveled, asking: "What kind of a man is this, that even the winds and the sea obey Him?" (v. 27)

Indeed, what kind of man is this who can calm the storm with a word? Who is this God who is willing to meet us in even the roughest seas of our life? One who invites the desperate to marvel, not just at His acts of deliverance, but in who He is. Peter later was commended for realizing who this carpenter was when he declared: "You are the Christ" (Mark 8:29).

Take time now to thank your Lord for a specific act of deliverance in a recent storm. Then, praise Him in prayer as you marvel at who He is—the Christ, the Son of the Living God.

Chapter 9

WHEN A LEADER FAILS

Numbers 20:1–13, 23–29

"Not many of you should presume to be teachers," James counsels in his letter, "because you know that we who teach will be judged more strictly" (James 3:1 NIV). Haven't you seen this to be true, especially regarding Christian leaders?

For example, if Hollywood stars cavort with someone other than their spouses, their box office appeal may suffer initially, but if they entertain us well enough, we make them our favorites again. However, if a reporter discovered a sordid story from Billy Graham's past, he'd be through. A double standard of judgment exists for spiritual leaders and the rest of the world. That standard is divinely intended.

How the Lord dealt with the Israelites when they failed and how He dealt with Moses in his failure prove this true.

At the Red Sea, the Israelites' knees shook, and in their fear they cried out until Yahweh parted the waters. At Massah and Meribah they demanded that Moses give them water, whining that he had led them into the desert, not to free them, but to kill them off (Ex. 17:1–7). After leaving Mount Sinai, they clamored for meat and treated God's manna with contempt (Num. 11:4–6). Finally at Kadesh, when the Israelites refused to trust God and enter the Promised Land, lobbying instead to elect a leader for the return trip to Egypt (14:1–4), Yahweh had had enough. He purged the faithless generation through forty more years of wandering. Yahweh endured a number of rebellious moments before He exacted punishment.

But for Moses—His leader, His chosen mediator, His faithful mouthpiece—only one infraction incurred God's irrevocable judgment.

Scripture refuses to airbrush its portraits, perhaps so that we will not be tempted to idolize the man over the Maker. If not for Numbers 20, we might put Moses on a pedestal. This chapter highlights the failure of a most revered scriptural hero and underscores the expectations God places on His leaders.

Return to Kadesh

At Kadesh almost forty years prior,[1] the previous generation trusted their fears over their faith (13:25–14:35). A generation that started with unbelievable promise ended with unfathomable sorrow. Rather than entering the land of the Lord's promise, they died off slowly over forty years of wilderness wandering.

Now their children returned to Kadesh, legs weary from wandering and hearts heavy from funerals. Few were left. Then Moses lost one more:

> Then the sons of Israel, the whole congregation, came to the wilderness of Zin in the first month; and the people stayed at Kadesh. Now Miriam died there and was buried there. (20:1)

Miriam. The sister who had followed the floating wicker basket that carried the baby Moses through the reeds and into the arms of Pharaoh's daughter (Ex. 2:1–10). This sister now died on her brother's watch. We might expect to read of Moses' grief, to hear the moans of a brother for a lost sister. Instead, without the opportunity to mourn, Moses heard an all-too-familiar moan of a hard-hearted people.

The "Got No Water" Blues, Reprised

> There was no water for the congregation, and they assembled themselves against Moses and Aaron. The people thus contended with Moses and spoke, saying, "If only we had perished when our brothers perished before the Lord! Why then have you brought the Lord's assembly into this wilderness, for us and our beasts to die here?" (Num. 20:2–4)

No water was nothing new (Ex. 17:1–3). The children sang the same refrain as their parents, blaming Moses rather than trusting Yahweh.

Moses was near or had just turned 120 years old.[2] At times, age has a tendency to shorten the fuse, thin the patience. Though grief-

---

1. Aaron's death later in the chapter places this event in the "fortieth year after the sons of Israel had come from the land of Egypt . . . in the fifth month" (Num. 33:38).

2. Six months later (Deut. 1:3), Moses wrote and delivered Deuteronomy to the Israelites shortly before his own death (34:7).

stricken and worn down by forty years of shepherding fickle and faithless people, Moses dropped to his knees before the Lord:

> Then Moses and Aaron came in from the presence
> of the assembly to the doorway of the tent of meeting
> and fell on their faces. (Num. 20:6a)

Moses, Spare the Rod

Yahweh had every right to judge the people for such fleeting faith. Instead, He instructed Moses to care for the flock:

> Then the glory of the Lord appeared to them; and
> the Lord spoke to Moses, saying, "Take the rod; and
> you and your brother Aaron assemble the congrega-
> tion and speak to the rock before their eyes, that it
> may yield its water. You shall thus bring forth water
> for them out of the rock and let the congregation
> and their beasts drink." (vv. 6b–8)

At first, Moses complied completely with the Lord's instructions. He took the rod, went with Aaron, and assembled the people (vv. 9–10a). On the surface, no cracks appeared. But underneath Moses simmered. He had bowed before the Lord in submission, but deep within, he was churning. While God desired to administer grace, Moses exploded like a once-dormant volcano:

> And he said to them, "Listen now, you rebels; shall
> we bring forth water for you out of this rock?" Then
> Moses lifted up his hand and struck the rock twice
> with his rod; and water came forth abundantly,
> and the congregation and their beasts drank.
> (vv. 10b–11)

Smack! Smack! Instead of speaking to the rock and refreshing Israel, Moses struck the rock and screamed at the people. Since God refused to unload His wrath, Moses unfurled his own attack.

Didn't they deserve it? Selfishly, they came with a faithless complaint to Moses, a man battered by grief over Miriam's death. Was Moses' response so wrong? After all, we may say, he was only human.

No Excuses, Moses

> But the Lord said to Moses and Aaron, "Because you
> have not believed Me, to treat Me as holy in the

sight of the sons of Israel, therefore you shall not bring this assembly into the land which I have given them." (v. 12)

One act of disobedience. One verse. One sentence. No appeals. Seem harsh? Let's examine the rationale of Yahweh. He cites two specific reasons here. We will also discover a third reason tucked away in the New Testament.

Barred from the Promised Land

First Indictment: Unbelief

God stated, "Because you have not believed Me . . ." What didn't Moses believe? He didn't believe God's words; he added to them. He didn't believe God's intention for grace; he administered wrath. He didn't believe God's spirit; he acted on his own flesh. Moses' job was not simply to mediate between God and Israel but also to model faith and trust in Yahweh. God expected His chosen leader to obey rather than acquiesce to his own angry emotions. Psalm 106:32–33 recounts Moses' lapse of judgment:

> They angered God again at Meribah Springs;
>   this time Moses got mixed up in their evil;
> Because they defied God yet again,
>   Moses exploded and lost his temper.[3]
> (THE MESSAGE)

While the sheep bleated and wandered, God's shepherd should have held fast to his higher calling.

Second Indictment: Desecration

Not only did Moses act out of unbelief, he also assaulted the very sanctity of God. The Lord told him that he did not "treat [Him] as holy in the sight of the sons of Israel." Out of control and under the influence of his flesh, he called the children of God "rebels" and took credit for the miracle: "Shall we bring forth water for you out of this rock?" Up until this point in his life, Moses had ascribed the miracles to the One true God. Here, instead of bringing glory to the Lord, he brought attention to himself and thus trampled on the holiness of God.

3. Eugene H. Peterson, The Message: The Wisdom Books (Colorado Springs, Colo.: NavPress, 1996), p. 229.

By speaking to the rock, Moses would have modeled the miraculous provision of the Lord. By striking it and focusing on his own ability, he supplanted Yahweh as the ultimate authority. As a leader, Moses was to be God's servant, not His strong arm.

Third Indictment: Battery

In his rash action, Moses not only struck the holiness of God, but he unwittingly spoiled the symbolic picture of Christ. Tucked away in 1 Corinthians, we read about God's intentions for that rock in the lonely desert:

> For I do not want you to be unaware, brethren, that our fathers were all under the cloud and all passed through the sea; and all were baptized into Moses in the cloud and in the sea; and all ate the same spiritual food; and all drank the same spiritual drink, *for they were drinking from a spiritual rock which followed them; and the rock was Christ.* (10:1–4, emphasis added)

Moses could never have known the intention of God to use a simple rock as a metaphor for Christ. To Moses, it was nothing more than a stone. To Yahweh, however, it embodied a future statement about His Son. In beating the rock, Moses inadvertently battered a symbol of Christ.

The Verdict

The seriousness of the verdict disclosed how seriously God took the crime. Moses was but a few miles and a few months away from finally entering the Promised Land (Deut. 34:1–7). But the Lord said no. Moses and Aaron would pass the baton to another leader and die on the fringe of Canaan. What a tragic mistake—one Moses could never undo no matter how much he wished to.

To make matters worse, the chapter that began with Miriam's death ends with Aaron's death:

> Then the Lord spoke to Moses and Aaron at Mount Hor . . . saying, "Aaron will be gathered to his people; for he shall not enter the land which I have given to the sons of Israel, because you rebelled against My command at the waters of Meribah. Take Aaron and his son Eleazar and bring them up to Mount

Hor; and strip Aaron of his garments and put them on his son Eleazar. So Aaron will be gathered to his people, and will die there." (Num. 20:23–26)

This time, "Moses did just as the Lord had commanded" (v. 27a). Moses transferred Aaron's priestly garments to Eleazar, passing the baton to the next generation. Then Aaron died, and "all the house of Israel wept for Aaron thirty days" (v. 29b). Moses lost both his siblings in a short span of time, and he lost his opportunity to lead Israel into the Promised Land.

As we'll see in the chapters that follow, however, the Lord still had work for even this fallen leader to do.

Fast-Forward to Today

God's punishment goes against the grain of an age that's passionate about explaining away leaders' foibles as "lapses in judgment" or "just human error." In our culture, many see God's judgment as too harsh. If we look at other examples of people vandalizing the Lord's sanctity, Moses' punishment was in reality a pardon.

For example, the Lord consumed Aaron's sons immediately after they desecrated the tabernacle (Lev. 10:1–3). Ananias and Sapphira lied to the Spirit and dropped dead (Acts 5:1–11). Even Miriam might have died from leprosy rather than old age if Moses had not interceded after she challenged the Lord's anointed (Num. 12:1–15). "They're only human" doesn't compete with "He is God."

While our culture more and more tries to hold political and business leaders to a lower standard, God continually calls His leaders to a higher plane. Spiritual leadership is not about fairness, being freed of responsibility, or finding personal glory. Spiritual leadership calls for obeying without question, modeling God's message regardless of society's logic, and giving up personal gain for God's glory.

If you find yourself being moved toward spiritual leadership, whether it be teaching two-year-olds or leading a Bible study or pastoring a church, apply these four characteristics of a spiritual leader to your life:

- Serve others patiently . . . even when they cause irritation.

- Obey God completely . . . even when the reason is unclear.

- Accept His plan willingly . . . even though you question it.

- Submit to the Lord continually . . . even when it hurts.

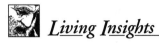 *Living Insights*

Why do we often feel like a volcano ready to spew its molten fire? From yelling at our kids to cursing at work to bullying others on the freeway, nothing seems to escape our anger. How do we corral this anger? Is all anger bad?

Both Moses and Jesus got angry. For Moses, anger led him to speak and act "rashly" (Ps. 106:33). In Jesus' case, He fashioned a whip and cleared the temple of greedy moneychangers (John 2:13–17). Christ acted out of righteous indignation; Moses simply acted out of indignation. Paul encourages us, "Be angry, and yet do not sin; do not let the sun go down on your anger, and do not give the devil an opportunity" (Eph. 4:26–27).

So next time you hear the rumbling of your volcanic anger, ask yourself and the Lord three questions:

- How can I diffuse my anger without sinning?

- If I bury this anger, will it simply fester?

- By acting out on this anger, what opportunity am I giving to Satan?

 Invitation to Worship

Perhaps you have failed in leadership—maybe morally, maybe miserably, maybe minutely. During those times, worship, much less talking to God, feels impossible. The breach is too great. After Nathan exposed David and his atrocious sins of adultery and murder, David wrote these words:

> Have mercy on me, O God,
>   according to your unfailing love;
> according to your great compassion
>   blot out my transgressions.
> Wash away all my iniquity
>   and cleanse me from my sin.
> For I know my transgressions,
>   and my sin is always before me.
> Against you, you only, have I sinned
>   and done what is evil in your sight,
> so that you are proved right when you speak

and justified when you judge. . . .
Create in me a pure heart, O God,
    and renew a steadfast spirit within me. . . .
Restore to me the joy of your salvation
    and grant me a willing spirit, to sustain me. . . .
O Lord, open my lips,
    and my mouth will declare your praise.
(Ps. 51:1–4, 10, 12, 15 NIV)

For David, the scars were permanent. He lost a child and tainted his reputation. Yet God's favor cleansed the wounds. Your scars may feel fresh, but your sins can never supplant the grace of God. For David, his worship of God began with repentance and ended with adoration.

Take the first step . . . confess to God with your own words:

_____

_____

_____

_____

_____

_____

_____

Take the next step . . . adore God for His mercy and grace:

_____

_____

_____

_____

_____

_____

Chapter 10

SAME SONG,
ELEVENTH VERSE . . .
HOPE BEYOND SNAKEBITE

Numbers 21:4–9; John 3:14–16

D o you sometimes wonder if your children will *ever* grow up? Doesn't it feel at times like they will remain forever in a state of perpetual adolescence? When God looked down at the second generation of Israelites as they left Mount Hor, He must have felt that way too. Though they had grown older, they didn't appear to be any wiser than their parents' generation.

Adult bodies but adolescent minds. Adult voices but adolescent speech. Adult ages but adolescent emotions. We learn from the Israelites that growing older does not necessarily mean growing up. Sometimes adults have to be disciplined like children in order to wake up to the grace of God.

A Different Direction . . . but the Same Refrain

On the outskirts of Canaan, the king of Arad captured some of the Israelites (Num. 21:1). So Israel asked for the Lord's help, and the second generation of Israel's warriors mobilized against Arad's forces, which blocked the southern route to the Promised Land (v. 2). Confident after their stunning victory (v. 3), they probably expected to march right into Canaan. Instead,

> they set out from Mount Hor by the way of the Red
> Sea, to go around the land of Edom. (v. 4a)

They turned around! Instead of marching north, they found themselves on the all too familiar route back to the Red Sea. In a flash, the victorious warriors turned against Moses' leadership— again:

> The people became impatient because of the journey.
> (v. 4b)

The wilderness was hot, dry, and rugged; the journey had been long—forty years, to be exact. In their minds, the time had come to seize the moment of victory and invade Canaan. They'd already defeated the first king, and now they wanted to capture a few more crowns before all was said and done. Their expectations, however, collided with God's plan. As the guiding cloud of His presence moved south, they became frustrated and angry, and they lashed out:

> The people spoke against God and Moses, "Why have you brought us up out of Egypt to die in the wilderness? For there is no food and no water, and we loathe this miserable food." (v. 5)

Sound familiar? Much like a broken record, the second generation carried the same tune as their parents. They turned on Moses—and by doing that, Yahweh Himself. Notice the audacity of their complaint.

First, they criticized God. Before, they had grumbled against Moses and/or Aaron (Ex. 14:11; 15:24; 16:2; 17:3; Num. 14:2; 16:41; 20:2–3) or murmured among themselves (11:1, 4, 10). Bad enough they contended against their leader who spoke with God face-to-face, but to vilify Yahweh along with His servant crossed the line.

Second, they lost sight of God's objective for them: "Why have you brought us up out of Egypt to die in the wilderness?" (21:5a). For forty years, the second generation buried their parents for similar accusations (see 14:2–4). God didn't bring them out of Egypt and secure victories over their enemies only to let them die in the desert. He had a land of promise waiting for them—a land *they* refused to enter forty years ago! Rather than trust Yahweh's direction, they relied on their finite perspective.

Third, they allowed their "overexposure" of God's grace to harden their hearts rather than soften them. "There is no food and no water," they whined. What were they thinking? The Lord had given them water from rocks, bread for two million mouths catered every morning, and quail till they got sick! The living God presided in the midst of His people, yet there they stood. Chins jutted out. Arms crossed. Hearts soured by discontentment.

Fourth, they despised God's grace. Pointing to the manna, the "bread of heaven" (Ps. 105:40), they dared to say, "We loathe this miserable food" (Num. 21:5b). In showing contempt for the Lord's provision, they showed contempt for the Lord. They had now blasphemed Yahweh.

A Divine Punishment . . . a Gracious Remedy

The Lord's displeasure at this was too great for words. Instead, He took immediate action:

> The Lord sent fiery serpents among the people and they bit the people, so that many people of Israel died. (21:6)

Their petulant whining turned to terrified screams. The venomous snakes poured into the camp, striking wildly at feet, legs, and hands. The pain of the snakebites was like fire as the poison burned through their veins. Many died an excruciating death.

Yet in God's grace, He spared some. Many—not all—died, even though they all deserved to. The Lord possessed the right to eradicate all who spoke against Him, but He didn't exercise that right. He gave the people a chance to come to their senses, which they rapidly did.

With snakes chasing them into their tents and friends writhing in mortal anguish, the Israelites quickly ascertained the gravity of their mistake:

> So the people came to Moses and said, "We have sinned, because we have spoken against the Lord and you; intercede with the Lord, that He may remove the serpents from us." And Moses interceded for the people. (v. 7)

The first step to growing up: owning our sin. The Israelites not only acknowledged their sin but accepted responsibility for it. They specifically identified how they pained the Lord and Moses.

In today's culture, apologies often avoid the full truth. People caught in flagrant sins or moral failures give the carefully crafted, prefabricated, catchall confession, "*If* I have done anything to cause pain, I am sorry." No personal recognition of sin is given, no owning of their transgressions. The Israelites took the first step toward maturity by humbling themselves before God and Moses and pleading for forgiveness.

Notice, too, Moses' position. The very people who had criticized him now begged for his mercy. He could have lectured them. He could have let them suffer as the snakes slithered and struck. He could have said, "See what happens when you mess with me!" But instead of getting even or lording his power over them, Moses dropped to his knees on their behalf. What a marked contrast to his anger at their grumbling at Meribah (20:10–11).

In His mercy, Yahweh provided a cure for the snake-stricken Israelites:

> Then the Lord said to Moses, "Make a fiery serpent, and set it on a standard; and it shall come about, that everyone who is bitten, when he looks at it, he will live." (21:8)

Instead of erasing the image of the poisonous reptiles from their minds, God desired to cement it in their memories. Moses did exactly what Yahweh told him:

> And Moses made a bronze serpent and set it on the standard; and it came about, that if a serpent bit any man, when he looked to the bronze serpent, he lived. (v. 9)

Pause for a moment to think about the aspects of Yahweh's mercy that this cure reveals.

First, He made an unlimited offer—anyone could receive the cure. Second, He designed the cure to be identical for everyone—all anyone had to do was look. Third, He provided a remedy complete in itself—all the people had to do was look, and they would be healed instantaneously. Finally, He made it simple—they didn't have to recite a prayer while looking at the bronze serpent or pledge perfect obedience from then on. They just had to look.

Relieved, restored, healed. Deserving punishment, they received God's grace.

A Past Example . . . a Present Reality

This story should certainly make us stop and think before we start complaining about our circumstances, shouldn't it? Yet we often take for granted and think too little of God's gracious direction and provision for our lives. What can we do to curb this natural tendency?

First, *we can cultivate a spirit of gratefulness*. As David wrote in Psalm 103: "Bless the Lord, O my soul, And forget none of His benefits" (v. 2). Recalling that good things come to us from God's goodness and love for us can help us avoid developing a sense of entitlement.

Second, *we can put ourselves on "grumble alert."* Most likely, we

aren't even aware of how much we grumble and complain throughout a day. Let's ask the Lord to help us pay more attention to the
words that pass our lips, the tone that carries them, and the heart
that prompts them.

Third, *we can train our eyes to see the Giver in the gifts.* We often
do this on the human plane, especially with our children. When a
child puts all his or her heart into a drawing for us that we can't
decipher no matter how hard we try, we look past the shapes and
colors to two bright eyes and see the love that motivated that gift,
don't we? We need to do the same thing with the Lord—training
our eyes to look beyond and through the gift to the One who has
lavished such love, grace, and generosity on us.

Just as we don't want our children to remain childish and adolescent forever, so the Lord wants us to grow up and become mature
believers who can relate more deeply with Him (see Heb. 6:1). He'd
rather not have to accomplish this through painful discipline—but
through the greatness of His grace. We're instructed to

> grow in the grace and knowledge of our Lord and
> Savior Jesus Christ. To Him be the glory, both now
> and to the day of eternity. Amen. (2 Pet. 3:18)

 Living Insights

Someone has said that if we gathered all the alleged pieces of
the cross that are for sale in the Holy Land, we could build a
battleship! Though the cross is long gone, people still crave a symbol, a token reputed to possess power. We hang onto religious
trinkets like they were Christian rabbits' feet. Sometimes we get so
attached to the symbol that we miss the message.

Seven hundred years after Moses fashioned the bronze serpent,
King Hezekiah had to destroy it.

> He removed the high places and broke down the
> sacred pillars and cut down the Asherah. He also
> broke in pieces the bronze serpent that Moses
> had made, for until those days the sons of Israel
> burned incense to it; and it was called Nehushtan.
> (2 Kings 18:4)

The symbol of salvation had become an idol! The people had

replaced the message with the image. They traded the Creator for the creation.

Are you hauling around any Nehushtans? Are there any Christian rabbits' feet in your life? Has some symbol of the faith—a cross, a picture of Jesus, even a Bible—replaced the Person of God in your attention and affection?

_____

_____

_____

_____

How do you think the Lord feels about this?

_____

_____

_____

_____

Christian relics are powerless to heal; worship styles are not sacred; ancient churches are not clothed with divinity; Bible knowledge alone cannot change a life. Only God heals; only God is worthy of our worship; only God can give us life. If all the churches of the world burned down, Yahweh would still be alive and well, residing in the people of God. The time is now to stop trusting the Nehushtans in our lives and start trusting the God who loves and saves us.

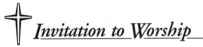 ## *Invitation to Worship*

Clandestine meetings often take place at night, when vision is blurred and identities shrouded. In this manner a Pharisee named Nicodemus approached a renegade rabbi known as Jesus in an effort to hide the meeting from his colleagues. With one statement, the Son of a carpenter transformed the teacher of the Law into a pupil: "Truly, truly, I say to you, unless one is born again he cannot see the kingdom of God" (John 3:3).

Taken aback, Nicodemus attempted in vain to reconcile physiology and theology: "How can a man be born when he is old? He cannot enter a second time into his mother's womb and be born, can he?" (v. 4). Jesus explained that one must be born again through repentance and regeneration of the Spirit. Brow furrowed, Nicodemus asked, "How can these things be?" (v. 9).

Jesus took him back to a familiar passage, easily recognized by one so learned in Hebrew Scriptures: "As Moses lifted up the serpent in the wilderness, even so must the Son of Man be lifted up; so that whoever believes will in Him have eternal life" (vv. 14–15).

The Israelites looked at the serpent and were healed. No questions, no assessment of their infractions, no pledge of future perfection. Jesus told Nicodemus that salvation is not about checking off good works, about praying a certain number of times each day, or about maintaining an appearance of purity. Salvation comes from simply looking at Jesus on the cross and believing He came, died, and rose again. As Paul tells us in Romans:

> If you confess with your mouth Jesus as Lord, and believe in your heart that God raised Him from the dead, you will be saved. (10:9)

Have you looked at Him? Have you recognized that your sin will lead toward eternal punishment and the only thing that can save you is Jesus' death on the cross?

If not, take a moment to pray this prayer. The prayer is not magical, just as the serpent was not magical, but it may help you get your thoughts started.

> *God, I know I have been living in rebellion against You. You have brought my sins before me, and I desire Your forgiveness. I believe in Your Son Jesus Christ, that He came, He died, and He rose again. I pray that You will come into my life and change me for Your purpose. Amen.*

Chapter 11
ALMOST HOME
Deuteronomy 6:1–13

They stood on the cusp of Canaan. Across the Jordan they saw their future home. The Israelites had spent forty years traversing an eleven-day journey.[1] Men dreamed about conquering armies and then cultivating land. Women imagined cooking something other than manna—and in their own kitchens. Kids wondered about what a "land of milk and honey" looked like. No more tent pegs. No more dust clouds from millions of walking feet. No more wandering. Israel looked over Jordan and envisioned a new country, new borders, and God's people establishing a home.

Moses, though, wouldn't be joining these people he had so faithfully led all these years. Instead, he would be turning over the reigns of leadership to Joshua. But before he did that, he had one more important job to do. He would deliver a series of sermons that would restate the terms of the covenant made forty years ago with the previous generation and renew it with the present generation. He would not be giving new information—only wisdom they would need that was grounded in the Law previously received.

This book, the book of Deuteronomy, contains the essentials of God's commands, the foundation of the Israelites' faith, and their road map for a new life.

Insight into Deuteronomy

Throughout the book of Deuteronomy, Moses reminded Israel of God's loving initiative toward them (see 7:7–9). He chose them, not because they were the mightiest, most impressive nation (which they weren't), but simply because He loved them and was determined to keep His promises to Abraham, Isaac, and Jacob. He was the One who brought them out of Egyptian slavery and misery. He was the One who brought them through the Red Sea and fed them in the wilderness. He was the One who would give them a land of their own and bless every aspect of their lives.

---

1. Deuteronomy 1:2 mentions the distance from Horeb, or Mount Sinai, to Kadesh-barnea, the first site of entering the Promised Land, as a journey of eleven days. This verse was a painful reminder of the price of disobeying Yahweh.

Though the initiative sprang from God's greatheartedness, He didn't want to be in a one-sided relationship. He wanted His people to love Him in return and show His glory to the nations. They would do this, Moses told them, through obeying the Lord and living in the path of life that His commands marked out.

Centuries later Jesus crystallized the basic theme of Deuteronomy:

> "If you love Me, you will keep My commandments." (John 14:15; see also 15:10; 1 John 5:3)

Hear, O Israel!

Following a review of God's care from the Exodus through the long wilderness wandering and a recapitulation of the Ten Commandments and Yahweh's fearsome presence at Sinai, Moses addressed Israel's present need.

> "Now this is the commandment, the statutes and the judgments which the Lord your God has commanded me to teach you, that you might do them in the land where you are going over to possess it, so that you and your son and your grandson might fear the Lord your God, to keep all His statutes and His commandments which I command you, all the days of your life, and that your days may be prolonged. O Israel, you should listen and be careful to do it, that it may be well with you and that you may multiply greatly, just as the Lord, the God of your fathers, has promised you, in a land flowing with milk and honey." (Deut. 6:1–3)

Did you catch the purpose at the heart of God's Law? "That your days may be prolonged . . . that it may be well with you . . . that you may multiply greatly." He wanted them to succeed, to prosper, to flourish, to be happy. The Lord doesn't stand over us with a club, waiting to smash us when we break His rules. No, that's not His heart. He wants to keep us from harm and lead us in the way of real life, or as Jesus said, "I came that they may have life, and have it abundantly" (John 10:10b).

The next few parts of Moses' sermon constructed four strong pillars to support the future life God wanted His people to lead. They became so significant to the Jewish people that they gave them a name, *Shema*, which means "hear." To this day, this is the most basic confession of faith for Jews all over the world.

"The Lord Is One!"

> "Hear, O Israel! The Lord is our God, the Lord is one!" (Deut. 6:4)

"Yahweh is our God—the one and only God!" Moses exclaimed, "Hear this, and let it ring in your memory continually!" Having come out of Egypt—with its pantheon of gods—and about to enter Canaan—with its multitude of idols—the Israelites needed to remember that Yahweh alone was the real God. They would need to turn to Him and no other for safety, for the success of their crops, for protection and victory over their enemies. This one sentence set the Israelites apart from all the other people of their day. Instead of worrying about which angry god to appease, they could rest secure in loving the one and only God, the only Creator of heaven and earth, the mighty Lord who loved them.

"Love the Lord Your God"

> "You shall love the Lord your God with all your heart and with all your soul and with all your might." (v. 5)

Moses next made it clear that the Israelites' worship of this unique God was centered on love, not laws. This love needed to come from their whole being. Commentator Ian Cairns helps us understand the totality that Moses was speaking of:

> To love Yahweh with the whole heart means to open to God all the processes of thinking, feeling, and deciding, to be shaped and honed as instruments aligned to God's purposes. . . .
> . . . to love with the [soul] means to place our feelings and desires at God's service and conform them to God's will.
> . . . [Might] is a single-minded, love-inspired zeal and determination to realize the whole will of God.[2]

---

2. Ian Cairns, *Word and Presence: A Commentary on the Book of Deuteronomy,* International Theological Commentary Series (Grand Rapids, Mich.: William B. Eerdmans Publishing Co., 1992), pp. 84–85.

This is how the Israelites were to love the Lord: fervently, with lives open to Him, placed at His service, and eager to do His will. They would best discover and understand His heart and will by meditating on His words:

> "These words, which I am commanding you today, shall be on your heart." (Deut. 6:6)

"Take them into your heart," Moses was saying, "and cherish them and let them guide your life."

"Teach Them Diligently to Your Sons"

The Lord's words, however, were not to be for personal devotions only; they were for the benefit of all generations to come:

> "You shall teach them diligently to your sons and shall talk of them when you sit in your house and when you walk by the way and when you lie down and when you rise up. You shall bind them as a sign on your hand and they shall be as frontals on your forehead. You shall write them on the doorposts of your house and on your gates." (vv. 7–9)

Fathers, mothers, and grandparents were commissioned to pass on the torch of spiritual life to their offspring. Would there be priests? Yes. Would the Levites preach? Yes. But Sabbath sermons were all too easy to forget during the week. More than seeking to convert the culture of Canaan, the Lord desired the Israelites to convert their own children.

Children in any generation will not be convinced of the truth unless they see it lived out in the dailiness of life. The Lord wants passion for Him to be exhibited hour-by-hour, not Sabbath-by-Sabbath.

> Relating to God is not a hobby, like taking up stamp-collecting or jogging; it is a total lifestyle. It means giving him wholehearted and unswerving loyalty all the time, putting time and effort into finding out what he wants and letting what he wants be the priority in family, business and social life.[3]

---

3. Mary Evans, "The Message of Deuteronomy," *The Bible for Everyday Life*, ed. George Carey (Grand Rapids, Mich.: William B. Eerdmans Publishing Co., 1996), p. 59.

As Moses presented it, the process of transferring truth was both intentional and natural. When they sat around the fire, they could recount the stories of Yahweh's deliverance. When they went for walks and witnessed a sunset, they could teach the young about the great Creator. At the dinner table, they could teach their children to appreciate God's graciousness. At bedtime, they could pray with their children and teach them to find rest in the Lord. The Lord and His ways were to naturally permeate every aspect of their lives. They were entrusted to translate Yahweh into everyday life.

"Fear Only the Lord Your God"

"Then it shall come about when the Lord your God brings you into the land which He swore to your fathers, Abraham, Isaac and Jacob, to give you, great and splendid cities which you did not build, and houses full of all good things which you did not fill, and hewn cisterns which you did not dig, vineyards and olive trees which you did not plant, and you eat and are satisfied, then watch yourself, that you do not forget the Lord who brought you from the land of Egypt, out of the house of slavery. You shall fear only the Lord your God; and you shall worship Him and swear by His name." (vv. 10–13)

Strange isn't it, that when the Lord lavishes blessings on us— things we took no part in accomplishing—we focus on our pleasure and security and forget about Him? Unbelievable as it is, we forget the Lord; it's part of human nature. This is why Moses addressed this tendency in the Israelites. As soldiers plotted battle plans, as newlyweds hoped for newborns, and as artisans developed business proposals, Moses wanted them to remember that victory rested not in weapons and that prosperity didn't depend on market research. Blessings depended on fearing and worshiping Yahweh only.

What does it mean to "fear the Lord"? Ian Cairns explains:

God's people are not to forget their experience of God's liberating grace (v. 12) nor God's jealousy (. . . the expression of consuming love; 4:24). Thus the "fear" is not a paralyzing recoil, but a reverential awareness of the responsibilities entailed in being so loved. "Fear" finds expression in "serving" ("worshiping") and in undivided loyalty. One "swears by" one's ultimate point of reference; so swearing by Yahweh is implicitly an acknowledgment that Yahweh is the focus of our personal and community life.[4]

"A reverential awareness of the responsibilities entailed in being so loved"—that's what would keep Israel, and us, mindful and grateful for the Lord's tender mercies.

Hear, O Christians!

Seeing the application to our lives today of this ancient, though always relevant, text isn't hard, is it?

First, we need to *hear the truth continually*. Always ringing in our minds should be the truth that the Lord is the only true God and the unity of Father, Son, and Holy Spirit. He is one in purpose and characteristics: coeternal, coexistent, coequal. Though we should treat people of other religions with the respect and love of Christ, no wiggle room exists on this foundational, basic truth.

Second, we need to *love the Lord fervently*. The Lord needs to be the top priority of our lives, the great love of our life. He doesn't want a time slot in our lives, a weekly appointment to keep. He desires our hearts, our souls, our minds, and our strength. We need a with-all-we-have mentality in our relationship with the Lord.

Third, we need to *teach the young diligently*. Many parents are intimidated at the thought of being the main resource for their children's spiritual development. Look again at what Moses told the Israelites about how to pass on a spiritual legacy—when they walked, when they rose, when they sat down after a long day. It's a natural process that can happen any time of the day, in any circumstance. And it can be as simple as praying with our children or writing out verses on note cards and slipping them into their lunches or taping them on their mirrors. We just need to be authentic in our own walk with God and consistent about our teaching, helping our children make the Lord and His love top priority for them too.

Finally, we need to *fear the Lord greatly*. This means keeping Him always in the forefront of our minds, not forgetting Him. Respecting His ways, not disobeying Him or laughing at sin. Honoring His name, not taking it in vain. Trusting His will, not discarding it for our own.

"Fearing the Lord" means waking up to His presence, revering Him, and living in the light of His great love for us.

4. Cairns, *Word and Presence*, p. 86.

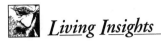 *Living Insights*

Nestled in the deep truths of Deuteronomy is the basic requirement of the Lord:

> "Now, Israel, what does the Lord your God require from you, but to fear the Lord your God, to walk in all His ways and love Him, and to serve the Lord your God with all your heart and with all your soul." (Deut. 10:12)

The prophet Micah rephrased this truth centuries later for his generation:

> He has told you, O man, what is good;
> And what does the Lord require of you
> But to do justice, to love kindness,
> And to walk humbly with your God? (Mic. 6:8)

Jesus heightened the standard of connection between God and people:

> "'You shall love the Lord your God with all your heart, and with all your soul, and with all your mind.' This is the great and foremost commandment. The second is like it, 'You shall love your neighbor as yourself.'" (Matt. 22:37b–39)

Most of the Old Testament Law has to do with the righteous treatment of other people. How does loving your neighbor as youself reflect your love for God?

_____

_____

_____

What does God's concern about how we treat each other reveal about His nature?

_____

_____

_____

How well are you loving the Lord? What would you like to change? What is one action you could do today to begin this process?

_____

_____

_____

How well are you sharing His love in tangible ways with the people He has put into your life? What is the Lord calling you to do now?

_____

_____

_____

✝ *Invitation to Worship*

Imagine the leader of your country walking into your house right now. You'd fumble around, throw the newspapers under the couch pillows, try to iron out the wrinkles in your shirt with your sweaty palms, and you would definitely stand to honor one of the most powerful people in the world. You would feel respect, awe, fear.

The Lord of the universe walks through our houses on a daily basis. Remember, if we are His children, He has promised to be with us. However, we often fail to pay Him the proper respect. We're not aware that He's there; we forget He is present.

Take some time right now to come before Him in prayer. Turn off the TV, the radio, or the music. Put away the newspaper, the mail, the book. Take some time to quiet your spirit and focus your mind. Ask the Lord to forgive you for breezing right by Him, for ignoring His love. Talk with Him from your heart. Ask His help to make you more aware of His presence, to deepen your understanding, acceptance, and responsiveness to His love.

Chapter 12

HOW TO KICK-START
A WHOLE NEW BEGINNING
Joshua 1:1–9

D on't we all sometimes wish that life would stand still? Most of us have a hard time with change—we feel safe with the familiar. A new job may bring higher pay and better benefits, but it also comes with new people, new procedures, a new commute, or even a new state. And definitely new anxieties.

Yet one thing is constant—change. As a traditional Jewish adage observes,

> Would that life were like the shadow cast by a wall
> or a tree, but it is like the shadow of a bird in flight.

How, then, can we become accustomed to and even succeed in a life fraught with transitions?

In the Lord's words to Joshua—new leader for a new land— we can find counsel and encouragement for handling the uncertainties in our own futures.

Six Guidelines to Kick-Start a New Beginning

For forty years, Israel had grown accustomed to one leader. Their ears knew when his voice was tinged with anger or laced with compassion. From Pharaoh's court to the Red Sea to the banks of the Jordan, his weathered face guided them. Moses was their shepherd, their lawgiver, and their mediator.

Then he died. Though he remained clear-eyed and strong to the end (Deut. 34:7), even he couldn't live forever. His sandals were not only hard to fill, they were impossible to fill. "Since that time no prophet has risen in Israel like Moses, whom the Lord knew face to face . . . and for all the mighty power and for all the great terror which Moses performed in the sight of all Israel" (vv. 10, 12).

How could Joshua compare? Sure, he was Moses' right-hand man, but his voice was unfamiliar, his style unknown. Was he really up to the task?

The Lord thought so, and that's all that mattered. From His

words to Joshua, we can draw out six principles that will also help us rise to the challenge of change.

Face Reality

> Now it came about after the death of Moses the servant of the Lord, that the Lord spoke to Joshua the son of Nun, Moses' servant, saying, "Moses My servant is dead." (Josh. 1:1–2a)

In those last five words, God told Joshua, "Moses died, I did not. I am very much alive. My very name, Yahweh, means 'I am.' Though your leader has perished, your mission has only begun."

Joshua was no longer the servant of Moses; he was the servant of Yahweh. By implication, the Israelites were commissioned to follow Joshua just as they had followed Moses.

Move On

> "Now therefore arise, cross this Jordan, you and all this people, to the land which I am giving to them, to the sons of Israel." (v. 2b)

All that they had been yearning for for forty years was now happening! No more waiting; no more wandering. Now was the time to enter the Promised Land, and the Lord told Joshua to lead them in. Yahweh charted out a new home for them and spread wide the boundaries (vv. 3–4). The time had come to move on and claim the promises of Yahweh.

Don't Be Afraid

> "No man will be able to stand before you all the days of your life. Just as I have been with Moses, I will be with you; I will not fail you or forsake you." (v. 5)

What a promise! Joshua didn't need to worry about being adequate for the task—Yahweh would support him. Whoever stood against Joshua stood against the living God! Yahweh guaranteed three things: His person, "I will be with you," His power, "I will not fail you," and His presence, "I will not forsake you." Joshua's leadership was established not on the basis of his résumé but on the guarantee of God.

Stand Tall

If God says something once, it's important. If He says it twice, it's significant. If He says it three times in a mere three verses, it's indispensable!

Once . . .

> "*Be strong and courageous*, for you shall give this people possession of the land which I swore to their fathers to give them." (v. 6, emphasis added)

Twice . . .

> "Only *be strong and very courageous*; be careful to do according to all the law which Moses My servant commanded you; do not turn from it to the right or to the left, so that you may have success wherever you go." (v. 7, emphasis added)

Three times . . .

> "Have I not commanded you? *Be strong and courageous*! Do not tremble or be dismayed, for the Lord your God is with you wherever you go." (v. 9, emphasis added)

The Lord moved the Israelites to reinforce His encouragement to Joshua. They pledged their obedience to their new leader:

> They answered Joshua, saying, "All that you have commanded us we will do, and wherever you send us we will go. Just as we obeyed Moses in all things, so we will obey you; only may the Lord your God be with you as He was with Moses. Anyone who rebels against your command and does not obey your words in all that you command him, shall be put to death; only *be strong and courageous*." (vv. 16–18, emphasis added)

Joshua and all Israel could stand tall in confidence because their courage was founded on God's promise to their forefathers. They would enter Canaan as strangers and remain as owners.

Stay Focused

"Be careful to do according to all the law which

Moses My servant commanded you; do not turn from it to the right or to the left, so that you may have success wherever you go." (v. 7b)

The Israelites were under new leadership, but not under new authority. They were not to forget the past but to build on it. Moses had led them to Canaan, Joshua was to lead them through the conquest, but God's Word would always remain constant:

"This book of the law shall not depart from your mouth, but you shall meditate on it day and night, so that you may be careful to do according to all that is written in it." (v. 8a)

As Israel's leader, Joshua would need to know Yahweh and His will in order to lead the people in it. They would follow his lead in choosing life or death, blessings or curses (see Deut. 28; 30:15–16, 19). Joshua's heart for God was crucial. If he led God's people in God's way, the Lord would give them "success wherever [they went]" (Josh. 1:7b).

Enjoy This

If Joshua would weave the Lord's law, which is "perfect . . . sure . . . right . . . pure . . . true . . . more desirable than gold" (Ps. 19:7–10), into the fabric of Israel's life, a tapestry of prosperity and success would pass down from generation to generation:

"For then you will make your way prosperous, and then you will have success." (Josh. 1:8b)

Once the mission was accomplished, the celebration could begin. God's intention all along was to reward His people with blessings, not because of their natural talents or their good works, but because they were His children.

A Concluding Thought

The first question of the Westminster Confession is "What is the chief end of man?" Many Christians might respond, "To go to church and be a good person." Instead, the confession answers, "To glorify God and *enjoy* Him forever."

We glorify Him in the same way that Joshua did—through trusting His Word, obeying His will, and being strong and courageous in our belief in Him. Joy comes from watching His faithfulness and care in our lives. "In every change He faithful will remain" the hymnwriter reminds us, adding these comforting thoughts:

> Be still, my soul! thy God doth undertake
> To guide the future as He has the past.
> Thy hope, thy confidence let nothing shake;
> All now mysterious shall be bright at last.
> Be still, my soul! the waves and winds still know
> His voice who ruled them while He dwelt below.[1]

 Living Insights

Darkness descended on the hill called Golgotha from noon until midday. His chest heaved, insults were hurled, and His heart broke under the weight of separation from His Father. Bearing the sin of mankind, Jesus cried out as His Father turned His head away. "'Eli, Eli, lama sabachthani?' . . . 'My God, My God, why have You forsaken Me?'" (Matt. 27:46b).

The word *forsake* indicates an intense form of abandonment. The holy God could not fellowship with sin, so the sinless Christ endured separation in our place. For us, abandonment is not an option. No matter how long the journey, no matter how difficult the change, God will never leave nor forsake us. Though discouraged when our children rebel against imparted truth, though embittered by an estranged spouse, though pained by the sudden loss of a friend, God remains changeless and near.

What hurt, pain, or change leaves you feeling desperate or discouraged?

_____

_____

_____

If you have not yet memorized Romans 8:31, make a flashcard:

> What then shall we say to these things? If God
> is for us, who is against us?

1. Katharina von Schlegel, "Be Still, My Soul," trans. Jane L. Borthwick in *The Hymnal for Worship and Celebration* (Waco, Tex.: Word Music, 1986), no. 347.

Eugene Peterson renders it in *The Message*, "With God on our side like this, how can we lose?"[2] Read Romans 8:31–39 and commit your struggle to the One who stands tall beside you.

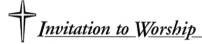

Invitation to Worship

Have you ever noticed how often the Lord encourages us to not be afraid? We are to fear—revere—Him, but not "tremble or be dismayed" at earthly circumstances, because "the Lord [our] God is with [us] wherever [we] go" (Josh. 1:9b).

Take some time now to meditate on the Lord's desire for us to be free from fear. Here are a few passages to get you started:

Psalm 56:4, 11	Luke 2:10–11
Psalm 118:5–6	Luke 12:32
Isaiah 44:6–8	Philippians 4:6–7
Daniel 10:12, 19	Hebrews 13:5–6
Matthew 14:26–27	1 Peter 5:6–7

End your time of study and meditation with prayer, taking your fears to the Lord and asking Him to give you courage and even excitement for whatever changes lie ahead of you.

---

2. Eugene H. Peterson, *The Message: The New Testament in Contemporary English* (Colorado Springs, Colo.: NavPress, 1993), p. 320.

Chapter 13

WATCHING THOSE WALLS TUMBLE DOWN

Selections from Joshua 6

God specializes in the impossible. He used a pebble in the sling of a shepherd to fell a battle-hardened giant (1 Sam. 17). He used a donkey to stymie a pagan prophet (Num. 22:21–35). With three hundred men and a skeptical leader (Judg. 7:1–8:10), Yahweh felled 120,000 swordsmen.

What fight do you face? Is there a fortress that feels impregnable right now? Perhaps your marriage has cooled to an amicable partnership. Maybe creditors stalk you like the FBI, and your debt recedes as fast as the polar caps. Or maybe your first child was born with a degenerative disease and you question the nearness of God.

When we face impossible odds, the temptation is to use our wits, our will, and our might to overcome the situation. But when we battle with temporal weapons, we miss out on a supernatural victory.

Impossible Odds

Chances are, you probably grew up hearing the story of the battle at Jericho. You know about the shouts, the trumpets, and you have sung songs about how the walls "came a tumblin' down." Some of us have grown so accustomed to the story that we have lost perspective of the dire straits facing the new leader of Israel.

While Israel camped on the other side of the Jordan, their spies came back to Joshua with a report on Jericho.

"Did you find anyone to help?" Joshua asked.

"We have one ally," they replied.

"Is he a government official? Is he a military general? Will he join us? Who can he influence?"

"No, *she's* a prostitute."

"Oh."

"But she welcomed us and assured us we can take the city."

"Alright. Return to your tribes and get your men ready" (see Josh. 2).

Joshua and the Israelites crossed the Jordan on dry land, as their parents had once crossed the Red Sea (3:7–17)! Then, they set up camp on the eastern side of Jericho. Joshua no doubt surveyed the city's wall, which was probably big enough for two chariots to ride abreast. The gates were tightly shut (6:1). No one came in, and no one came out. Even if they could get through such a wall, the losses would be huge. Furthermore, this generation of Israelites had won only two battles and none against such a fortress. The walled city taunted any attackers, "Try me. You'll lose." It was impregnable. Intimidating. Impossible.

Joshua turned to see a soldier brandishing a drawn sword. He was obviously separated from his troops, so Joshua approached the mystery man, "Are you for us or for our adversaries?" (5:13). The man turned, eyes burrowing into Joshua's heart, his voice deeply confident, "No; rather I indeed come now as captain of the host of the Lord" (v. 14a).

Joshua fell to the ground, and reminiscent of God speaking to Moses at the burning bush, the man said, "'Remove your sandals from your feet, for the place where you are standing is holy.' And Joshua did so" (v. 15b).

Donald Campbell observes:

> This was a deeply significant experience for Joshua. He had anticipated a battle between two opposing armies, Israelite and Canaanite. He had thought this was to be his war and that he was to be the general-in-charge. But then he confronted the divine Commander and learned that the battle was the Lord's. The top general of the Lord's army had not come to be an idle Spectator of the conflict, or even an ally. He was in complete charge and would shortly reveal His plans for capturing the citadel of Jericho.
>
> How comforting all this was for Joshua. He did not need to bear the heavy burden and responsibility of leadership alone. By removing his sandals he gladly acknowledged that this battle and the entire conquest of Canaan was God's conflict and that he was merely God's servant.[1]

1. Donald K. Campbell, "Joshua," *The Bible Knowledge Commentary*, Old Testament edition, ed. John F. Walvoord and Roy B. Zuck (Wheaton, Ill.: Victor Books, 1985), p. 339.

An Improbable Solution

Barefoot, down on his knees, the leader of Israel recognized the sovereignty of the living God:

> The Lord said to Joshua, "See, I have given Jericho into your hand, with its king and the valiant warriors." (Josh. 6:2)

What appeared impossible to Joshua was a definite reality in God's mind. As Campbell comments, "The tense of the Hebrew verb is prophetic perfect (I have delivered), describing a future action as if it were already accomplished. Since God had declared it, the victory was assured."[2] However, the victory relied on Yahweh's orders, not Joshua's. In humility, Joshua received a plan to take the city—one that would require this battle-tested soldier to sheathe his sword and warm up his vocal chords.

> "You shall march around the city, all the men of war circling the city once. You shall do so for six days. Also seven priests shall carry seven trumpets of rams' horns before the ark; then on the seventh day you shall march around the city seven times, and the priests shall blow the trumpets. It shall be that when they make a long blast with the ram's horn, and when you hear the sound of the trumpet, all the people shall shout with a great shout; and the wall of the city will fall down flat, and the people will go up every man straight ahead." (Josh. 6:3–5)

Yahweh unveiled a plan to accomplish the impossible with the unthinkable! Instead of ladders, the Lord commissioned trumpets. Instead of swords, Yahweh ordered shouts. Instead of charging the city, Israel was commanded to march around it. Joshua might have thought, *Now with Moses, You humiliated Pharaoh and his people with plagues. You proved Your might by parting the Red Sea and swallowing up the greatest army of the known world. But now You want us to march and shout and make music? Jericho will laugh us back to Egypt.*

However, like an unquestioning soldier, Joshua relayed the battle plans and began issuing orders to his people (vv. 6–11). In this battle, being stronger or smarter wasn't the goal—being obedient was.

---

2. Campbell, "Joshua," p. 340.

The Ridicule and the Rubble

Joshua 2:9–11 records that word had reached Jericho regarding the mighty acts the Lord had done for His people. Surely, when the Israelites marched out in full regalia, the people of Jericho cowered behind their walls. But what would they think as the days wore on?

Day one (6:11). The elite forces marched in front of the ark, which was carried by the priests who blew the trumpets, and the rear guard followed. As the trumpets blew, the armies of Jericho stiffened their spines, expecting the imminent attack. When Israel walked away without so much as a whisper, their enemies' curiosity replaced their fear.

Day two (v. 12–14a). Here they came again, just like the day before. Silent as cats, this invading army must have looked like they were performing a dirge. Instead of brandishing ladders and swords, they blew their horns, took a walk around the city, and returned to their tents.

Days three through six (v. 14b). After the sixth day of such a spectacle, no doubt the people of Jericho scoffed at Israel's "mighty" army. "Hey, you'll wear out your sandals walking around like that!" Laughter rained down from the ramparts. As the Israelites returned to their camps, some must have thought, *What are we doing? We look like fools. Imagine what the Canaanites were thinking—Watch out for those Israelites, they sure can march well! At least their trumpet section is good.*

Day seven (vv. 15–21). The Israelite army rose early just as it had on the six previous days. They marched once around the city just like before. But instead of retreating to camp, this time the Israelites kept going on their circuitous route.

After seven times, no doubt the people of Jericho were overwhelmed with curiosity. Suddenly the Israelites halted. The priests blew the horns. Then the voices of two million strong roared through the midmorning haze. Trumpets joined the cacophony. Reverberations shook the stones.

Some of the people of Jericho covered their ears at the unnerving symphony of noise. Then their legs gave way, and for a moment they felt weightless. They went from standing to falling to crashing on broken stone. Sharp pain coursed through their joints. Limbs crumpled on impact. Aching confusion replaced curiosity. *What happened? . . . the walls . . . ?* They tried to extract themselves from the rubble, but they were pinned by beams, trapped under stone, or dazed in shock. The shouts and trumpets continued to blare in the background of their minds, but then charging feet rushed by; the glint of a drawn sword appeared and for a moment blocked the sun. Darkness.

The walls fell flat, just as Yahweh had said. Impossible odds were overcome by an improbable solution. The fortress was leveled, the scoffers were muted, and God was exalted.

What Walls Intimidate You?

In these days of self-absorbed effort and humanly-energized strategies, the point to realize is that being stronger or looking smarter is not important when it comes to the big fights in life—turning it over to Him who will never face an impossibility is!

What Jericho-like situation faces you? What looks "tightly shut" (6:1) and seems too much for you to tackle? Not all of us have the same "Jericho" to face, but we all have two tendencies that will trip us up:

- Our nature to fight strength with greater strength

- Our nature to try to outsmart our opponents and put them down in an impressive way

Our nature, however, is not God's way. When you face a battle too big for you, remember these three truths:

First, *the battle we face is not difficult because of size or circumstance—it's difficult because it feels so impossible.* We should not deny the circumstances or the struggle, but we should recognize that our perspective is limited. *Impossible* is not in the Lord's vocabulary. God desires to reveal His strength through our weakness. Through our submission, He will succeed.

Second, *the plan we're to follow is not a struggle because it's complicated or confusing—it's a struggle because it seems so strange.* Walking by faith does not come as naturally as walking by sight. People will ridicule us for trusting in the Lord rather than trusting in ourselves. A plan of faith will, by definition, place us in realms of uncertainty. But in such strange surroundings, we will experience the supernatural.

Third, *the victory we need is not accomplished because of strength or smarts—it's accomplished because it is of God!* Remember what the Lord tells us in His Word: "'Not by might nor by power, but by My Spirit,' says the Lord of hosts" (Zech. 4:6b). "The righteous will live by his faith" (Hab. 2:4b). "Behold, I am the Lord, the God of all flesh; is anything too difficult for Me?" (Jer. 32:27).

Remember, God uses the unusual to do the impossible. Why? So our faith might shift from the horizontal to the vertical. Then He becomes our all in all, and He gets the glory He so richly deserves!

 Living Insights

If there was one man who could rely on his brain in a tough situation, it was Paul. Trained by the Ivy League schools of his day, endowed with the right pedigree, gifted with an ability to shift from philosophy to theology without grinding any gears, and connected with all the right people, Paul was a giant equipped with powerful weapons.

It was God who fought Paul's battles, and God who got the glory! But Paul maintained that any gifts or pedigree he possessed were rubbish compared to his relationship with Christ (Phil 3:4–9). From shackles in a prison to snakebites on a marooned island, Paul faced the impossible almost on a daily basis. When faced with battles, Paul spurned the flesh and put confidence in God's weapons:

> The truth is that, although of course we lead normal human lives, the battle we are fighting is on the spiritual level. The very weapons we use are not those of human warfare but powerful in God's warfare for the destruction of the enemy's strongholds. (2 Cor. 10:3–4 PHILLIPS)

Are you facing a battle right now? What is it?

_____

_____

_____

Are you tempted to depend on something within your own power rather than turning to the Lord? If so, on what do you depend most often—your intellect, your willpower, your connections with people, or something else?

_____

What has been the outcome? What happened to your "enemy"? What happened to you? What happened to the Lord's glory?

_____

_____

_____

Reflect on how the Lord fights battles. What spiritual and powerful weapons do you think He wants you to use instead of what you've tried so far?

_____

_____

_____

Commit now in prayer to seeking the Lord's plan for victory rather than depending first on your own strengths.

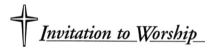

Invitation to Worship

When Hudson Taylor, the famous missionary, first went to China, it was in a sailing vessel. Very close to the shore of cannibal islands the ship was becalmed, and it was slowly drifting shoreward unable to go about, and the savages were eagerly anticipating a feast.

The captain came to Mr. Taylor and besought him to pray for the help of God. "I will," said Taylor, "provided you set your sails to catch the breeze." The captain declined to make himself a laughing stock by unfurling in a dead calm. Taylor said, "I will not undertake to pray for the vessel unless you will prepare the sails." And it was done.

While engaged in prayer, there was a knock at the door of his stateroom. "Who is there?" The captain's voice responded, "Are you still praying for wind?" "Yes." "Well," said the captain, "you'd better stop praying, for we have more wind than we can manage."[3]

Most people would scoff and say, "The wind would have come anyway." In an era in which logic and rationalism reign, little room remains in our psyche for the supernatural. When we hear about "miracles," often our first reaction is one of skepticism. Perhaps the reason why fortresses feel so impossible to conquer is because we don't really believe God is capable of handling the impossible. *That's not something He does today,* we think.

As you pray and seek God for a plan to reduce to rubble the walls in your life, are you ready to march in like Joshua when they come down? The Israelites were not paralyzed with shock that the walls came down; they immediately took action. Imagine for a moment a healed marriage, restored relationships, or a prodigal child returning home. Are you ready to worship God for His miracle in your life? Or to put it like Hudson Taylor, "Are your sails ready?"

---

3. As quoted by Paul Lee Tan, *Encyclopedia of 7,700 Illustrations* (Rockville, Md.: Assurance Publishers, 1979), no. 1493.

Chapter 14

DEFEAT ON THE
HEELS OF VICTORY
Selections from Joshua 7

Judah. What does the term bring to mind? Christ, the Lion of the tribe of Judah. Strength. Royalty. The father of the Davidic and Messianic line.

At the time of Christ, many Judahs were running around. The Greek transliteration of the name *Judah* was *Judas*. One Judas fueled the great Jewish revolt against the Syrians around 167 B.C.[1] One was the brother of Jesus. Two of them were among the first disciples. One possessed the surname Iscariot and betrayed Jesus with a kiss for thirty pieces of silver. That one sin not only secured his tragic end, but also smeared his name for the rest of history. One act of betrayal can bring shame to a name forever.

Joshua 7 contains the story of one man whose choices have caused his name to live in infamy. His story dramatically illustrates that the principles found in God's Word always prove to be true. People reap what they sow (Gal. 6:7). Sins done in private will be made public (Num. 32:23). "The eyes of the Lord are in every place/ watching the evil and the good" (Prov. 15:3). Unfortunately, these principles are learned through failure more often than through victory.

On a day when the Israelites should have been rejoicing in victory, they returned bloodied and defeated from the battle of Ai. One man had privately sown seeds of greed and caused Israel to bear the brunt of God's judgment. Though this man didn't intend to lead his country into an ambush, his one act of betrayal and disobedience directly led to Israel's only defeat in the conquest of the land of Canaan.

Everything Going According to Plan

As you might imagine, at this time, troop morale was at an all-time high. The city of Jericho had just fallen flat. Its rich spoils

---

1. Judas Maccabeus, the third of five sons of Mattathias, led the Jewish revolt against Antiochus Epiphanes IV, who desecrated the Jewish temple in 167 B.C.

had been collected to fill the Lord's treasury to overflowing. The fortress that had once kept out invading armies had been reduced to rubble, and Israel had annihilated many of the forces of Canaan. Word began to spread of the "miracle at Jericho," and armies trembled at the sight of Israel and their ark.

Once Jericho was destroyed, the march was on to the next destination. Ten miles northwest near Bethel stood a small village known as Ai. Joshua commissioned some men to spy out the city and survey its defenses. Bolstered by their recent victory, the spies confidently boasted:

> "Do not let all the people go up; only about two or three thousand men need go up to Ai; do not make all the people toil up there, for they are few." (Josh. 7:3b)

Though Joshua had thirty thousand elite forces on hand (8:3), the spies recommended only "two or three thousand." If God had given them a great walled city in seven days, surely this little village would take but seven minutes! So the Israelite forces marched up and engaged the enemy. However, instead of swaggering back home with whoops and hollers after a swift victory, the soldiers fled Ai with screams of terror:

> So about three thousand men from the people went up there, but they fled from the men of Ai. The men of Ai struck down about thirty-six of their men, and pursued them from the gate as far as Shebarim and struck them down on the descent, so the hearts of the people melted and became as water. (7:4–5)

On the heels of a major victory came a bitter defeat. Rejoicing was turned to mourning. Hearts of steel melted in the fire of despair. The hand of Yahweh's favor was suddenly removed. The wounded scuffled by Joshua, heads down. Women who had woken up that day as wives now wailed as widows. All eyes were on Joshua, asking, *How could God let this happen?*

A Desperate Plea

Dazed, dejected, and desperate, Joshua and his council fell to their knees:

> Then Joshua tore his clothes and fell to the earth

on his face before the ark of the Lord until the
evening, both he and the elders of Israel; and they
put dust on their heads. (v. 6)

In chapter 5, Joshua had fallen down before the Captain of the
Host in worship and homage. Here, he and his leaders unanimously
dropped down in shock and hopelessness.[2] Lying prostrate before
the ark with torn tunics and shrouded in dust,[3] Joshua pleaded to
know why Yahweh had abandoned His people (Josh. 7:7–9).

Some commentators believe Israel suffered defeat due to sinful
pride, underestimating their enemy, and outnumbering themselves
at least two to one.[4] However, the odds had never meant anything
to Yahweh. The Israelite warriors were confident because of God's
covenant promise, not their own ability. Even if Ai had been de-
fended with a full force of chariots and Israel had attacked with
only a handful of shepherd boys with slings, God's people could
still have claimed the victory. So what went wrong?

A Little Word with Huge Ramifications

The book of Joshua reads like a war journal. One can imagine
General Joshua sitting in his tent by candlelight, chronicling the
exploits, victories, and challenges faced by the Israelite people. By
the time the book of Joshua was finished, much of the conquest
had been completed. The rest of the task would fall to someone
other than Joshua.

This book serves as a testimony to the faithfulness of God and
an exhortation to Israel to finish what they started. While Joshua 6
rings with vigor and cheers, the very next chapter serves as a warning to the next generation of warriors: "As you finish this divinely
appointed job, don't let this ever happen again." The battle of Ai
was Israel's only defeat. When the author wrote this passage, he

2. Trent C. Butler, "Joshua," *Word Biblical Commentary* (Dallas, Tex.: Word Books, 1998),
vol. 7, accessed through the Logos Library System.

3. "Extreme grief was expressed by tearing the garments and placing dust upon the head,"
according to D. F. Payne. *New Bible Dictionary*, 2d ed., ed. J. D. Douglas and others (Wheaton,
Ill.: Tyndale House Publishers, Inc., 1982), p. 416.

4. Donald K. Campbell notes that because "Ai had 12,000 men and women, or about 6,000
men (8:25). . . . Israel was guilty of underestimating the strength of her enemy and of
overestimating her own strength." "Joshua," *The Bible Knowledge Commentary*, Old Testament
edition, ed. John F. Walvoord and Roy B. Zuck (Wheaton, Ill.: Victor Books, 1985), p. 344.

was quick to tell the reader the reason for this tragic event. One rejoices with Joshua's victory speech at the end of chapter 6, and then abruptly stumbles over the very next word.

"But . . . ." (7:1)

As ominous as a word could be, this one foreshadowed the disaster that would follow. Chapter 7 describes the actions of a man named Achan, who will forever be remembered for committing a tragic sin that contaminated the whole camp.

> But the sons of Israel acted unfaithfully in regard to the things under the ban, for Achan, the son of Carmi, the son of Zabdi, the son of Zerah, from the tribe of Judah, took some of the things under the ban, therefore the anger of the Lord burned against the sons of Israel. (v. 1)

Earlier in the narrative, Joshua had shouted instructions before Israel charged the city of Jericho. The spoils of victory belonged solely to the One who secured the victory—Yahweh Himself. Any precious items made of gold, silver, bronze, or iron were considered holy and reserved for God (6:19). Joshua had made this very clear to the sons of Israel:

> But as for you, only keep yourselves from the things under the ban, so that you do not covet them and take some of the things under the ban, and make the camp of Israel accursed and *bring trouble on it*. (6:18, emphasis added)

Note the word *trouble* here. This little term is crucial to the narrative of Joshua. Here, it gives us a clue about the events to follow concerning Achan, whose name in Hebrew literally means "trouble"! We will certainly see how much trouble he brings to Israel by the time all is said and done.

While the Israelites danced with joy, Achan scampered to his tent with a stockpile of gold, silver bars, and a beautiful, expensive garment (7:21). He actually stashed a curse rather than a costly treasure. Unbeknownst to Joshua, who was confidently preparing to send his troops into battle, Yahweh was preparing to execute His judgment on the people due to Achan's sinful disobedience.

Yahweh Speaks

Joshua fell on his face before the Lord. In Joshua's mind, Yahweh had broken His covenant with His people by allowing this bitter defeat to come upon them. Joshua cried out, "Alas, O Lord God, why did You ever bring this people over the Jordan, only to deliver us into the hand of the Amorites, to destroy us?" (v. 7b). Joshua's questions implied that the fault lay with God. However, like a well-trained surgeon, the Lord cut quickly to the heart of the problem:

> So the Lord said to Joshua, "Rise up! Why is it that you have fallen on your face? Israel has sinned, and they have also transgressed My covenant which I commanded them. And they have even taken some of the things under the ban and have both stolen and deceived. Moreover, they have also put them among their own things." (vv. 10–11)

Notice the intensity of the Lord's command: "Stop praying and get to your feet! It's time to act and face reality!" Notice, too, that the Lord does not single out one man, but the whole nation. One individual's secret sin brought great calamity upon his entire community. After alerting a stunned Joshua, Yahweh instructed him on how to go through the camp and identify the guilty party (vv. 13–15).

Joshua followed Yahweh's directions expediently and to the letter. The Lord commanded him to get up in the morning, so Joshua arose early and made the whole nation get up with him (v. 16). He narrowed down all the tribes to that of Judah, then the families down to the Zerahites, then the heads of the families down to Zabdi, and to his son Carmi, and then Joshua stepped before the trembling, uncomfortable, very guilty son of Carmi, Achan (vv. 16–19). Achan was proving to live up to his name—"trouble."

Achan's Response

As Joshua peered at Achan, no doubt the eyes of the whole community rested upon him as well. Achan felt not only the weight of his sin, but the yoke of his nation's defeat. He must have seen staring at him the haggard faces of newly widowed women and the sad eyes of now-fatherless children.

> Then Joshua said to Achan, "My son, I implore you, give glory to the Lord, the God of Israel, and give

praise to Him; and tell me now what you have done. Do not hide it from me." (v. 19)

Caged in guilt, Achan could have lied or blamed God for the temptation. Instead, he came clean:

> So Achan answered Joshua and said, "Truly, I have sinned against the Lord, the God of Israel, and this is what I did: when I saw among the spoil a beautiful mantle from Shinar and two hundred shekels of silver and a bar of gold fifty shekels in weight, then I coveted them and took them; and behold, they are concealed in the earth inside my tent with the silver underneath it." (vv. 20–21)

Not only did he recognize his sin, but his confession perfectly outlined the progression of temptation to sin. "I saw . . . I coveted . . . I took . . . I concealed." Though his ears heard the warnings of Joshua, when his eyes alighted upon the glittering spoils, Achan sowed seeds of greed. While every other warrior walked by the treasures reserved for God, he coveted them.

The reality of impending judgment, the threat of consequences, and Yahweh's disappointment dissolved in Achan's mind. He might have tried to rationalize the larceny by saying to himself: *God has plenty. Surely this little bit won't matter. It's not for me; I am doing it for my family. I'll tithe it back once we get settled in the land.* Lust replaced reason. Temporary financial gain replaced holiness. He believed the same lie the serpent told Eve: "Go ahead! It won't matter to God."

Israel's Response

Joshua sent messengers to Achan's tent, and they retrieved the plunder (vv. 23–24). Before the whole community, Joshua unveiled Achan's secret stash. One man's private sin was now made public. Imagine how the gold must have dulled in his mind, how the silver tarnished, and the garment cheapened before his eyes. Priceless treasures suddenly turned into worthless trinkets when lives were at stake. Achan would have traded everything to get one moment back—the moment when he should have walked on instead of lingering before the glittering temptation.

The Israelite people, laden with stones, encircled Achan's family, his sons, his daughters, and his livestock. Then Joshua delivered the death sentence:

> Joshua said, "Why have you troubled us? The Lord will trouble you this day." And all Israel stoned them with stones; and they burned them with fire after they had stoned them with stones. (v. 25)

Israel erected a mound of stones and called the valley Achor, or Trouble (v. 26). The tragedy that occurred there served as a powerful reminder that one man's actions could bring calamity upon the whole community. Furthermore, Achan's name took its place in infamy alongside the likes of Cain, Jezebel, and Judas.

Lingering Lessons

At the time of the conquest of the land of Canaan, two mounds of stones were erected near Jericho. One commemorated God's power of deliverance (Josh. 4:5–7), and the other warned of falling into the sin of Achan. These stone altars left lingering lessons that continue to warn us.

- **Lingering Lesson 1**—Surprising and strange defeats can often be traced back to secret sins.

- **Lingering Lesson 2**—Very private sins can lead to very public consequences.

- **Lingering Lesson 3**—Temptation blinds us to reality and makes us ignore the consequences.

- **Lingering Lesson 4**—Sweeping acts of disobedience call for severe responses of discipline.

Unfortunately, we often hear of successful Christian leaders whose private addictions to pornography or sex have become public. Their surreptitious sins have left an indelible scar on their ministries and families. To stay above reproach, some pastors keep a list of every consequence associated with such a fall. When tempted, they quickly pull it out and read through each point. Consequences of falling into sin include the loss of respect and reputation, the unfathomable pain inflicted upon spouse and children, a compromised testimony, loss of job and ministry, and public shame. When tempted, we need to open our eyes and consider the consequences of sin.

However, secret sins are not based solely in the sensual realm. A mom portrays a Cleaver household to the PTA but motivates her children to perfectionism through anger. A man teaches a Sunday school class on stewardship but gambles online profusely. A college student proudly displays her dean's list honors but hides her cheat sheets. We need to remember that "the eyes of the Lord move to and fro throughout the earth" (2 Chron. 16:9a). "Do not be deceived, God is not mocked; for whatever a man sows, this he will also reap" (Gal. 6:7). Though our sin may remain hidden under careful layers, God sees through our masks. His silence is not to be confused with approval. Rather, His silence gives evidence of His grace. He is waiting for us to return before it's too late.

 Living Insights

Though the Israelites lost this battle, Ai was eventually captured. Yahweh again gave these instructions to Israel after they had defeated the king: "You shall take only its spoil and its cattle as plunder for yourselves" (Josh. 8:2). If only Achan had waited twenty-four hours! Gold, silver, garments, and livestock would all have been his if he had simply obeyed the Lord. God will grant us the desires of our hearts, but in His timing, way, and means—not ours. Trouble surfaces when we seek to fulfill our desires outside of His plan.

Benjamin Franklin once said, "It is easier to suppress the first desire than to satisfy all that follow it."[5] Ultimately, material wealth and earthly temptations will never satisfy—they will only leave us hungry for more. The book of James sums up this way the progression from temptation to sin:

> But each one is tempted when he is carried away and enticed by his own lust. Then when lust has conceived, it gives birth to sin; and when sin is accomplished, it brings forth death. (James 1:14–15)

What temptations do you face on a regular basis?

_____

_____

5. Paul Lee Tan, *Encyclopedia of 7,700 Illustrations* (Rockville, Md.: Assurance Publishers, 1979), no. 6537.

_____

_____

_____

_____

_____

How does temptation progress to sin in your life?

_____

_____

_____

_____

_____

_____

In order to help suppress that first desire before it gives way to sin, create a covenant with a trusted friend whom you can call any time you find yourself in a difficult or tempting situation—morning, noon, or night. Pray that the Lord will strengthen you as you evaluate your thought processes and make a plan to resist temptation. Remember, it is through His power that you are set free (see Zech. 6:4 and James 4:7)!

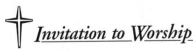 *Invitation to Worship*

When given the opportunity, Achan confessed his sin. He still incurred harsh punishment, but he came clean before God. Biblically, cleansing must precede worship. One is unable to worship a holy God with a tainted heart. If you find yourself going to church, singing songs, praying, and reading Scripture but you are harboring a secret sin, realize you are just doing lip service to God. Worship requires holiness.

When Isaiah was ushered before the throne and witnessed heavenly beings worshiping God singing, "Holy, Holy, Holy, is the Lord of hosts," his first response was painful recognition of his own sinfulness (see Isa. 6:3b). "Woe is me, for I am ruined! . . . I am a man of unclean lips . . . For my eyes have seen the King, the Lord of hosts" (v. 5b). Before he lingered any longer in the presence of God, a seraph purged his sin by touching a burning coal to Isaiah's lips (vv. 6–7).

Worship requires holiness. Holiness may require purging sin from your life. Sometimes, as with Isaiah, that process can be painful. But God desires your worship. You were created to love, obey, honor, and worship Him. Confess your sin to Him. If necessary, make amends with those who have been affected by your sin. Making it right may be painful or uncomfortable. But until your sin is purged, your worship is futile. Come to God with a humble heart, and He will restore you to fellowship with Him.

Chapter 15

THE SECRET:
AN ATTITUDE OF FORTITUDE
Joshua 14:6–14

At forty, many of us feel old. At sixty, we hit retirement and post signs saying, "Gone fishing," "Out of the office," and "My other car is a couch." Our culture purports the idea that since we worked for full-time pay, at sixty-five, it's time for full-time play.

However, we're hard pressed to find in the Bible the modern concept of "retirement." Surely, we should rest from our labors, but if we apply the present retirement paradigm, Sarah never would have entertained changing diapers at ninety. Instead of herding Hebrews to Canaan, Moses would have retired from herding sheep at eighty. And the apostle John would have vacationed on the island of Patmos rather than penned the last book of Scripture.

Once retired, many people suffer from feelings of uselessness, self-pity, fear, and guilt. These internal weights often sink hearts into deep depression. Retirees question their purpose and begin to wonder why life feels so empty. In this chapter, we will survey the life of one man who chose to trade in his rocking chair for a pair of hiking boots and to live his life to the fullest.

The conquest of the land of Canaan was coming to a close. The campaign against the Canaanites had been waging for five years.[1] The wanderers-turned-warriors were soon to become land-owning worshipers; Joshua stood poised to parcel out the land Yahweh promised them through Moses (Josh. 14:5). However, one region had yet to be defeated. One foe stood defiantly against the armies of God. In Joshua 14:6–14, nine verses recount the story of Caleb, an eighty-five-year-old man needing to settle a score and claim a forty-five-year-old promise (Num. 14:24; Deut. 1:36).

---

1. Caleb states that the Lord had let him live for forty-five years since they spied out the land the first time (Josh. 14:10). The Israelites wandered for forty years before crossing the Jordan. That leaves five years of fighting the Canaanite forces.

A Deed to the Land

Joshua was parceling the land out to the tribes of Israel (Josh. 13:7–33). Instead of waiting their turn, a group of men approached Joshua: "The sons of Judah drew near to Joshua in Gilgal" (14:6a). Parting the eager men, a crusty old warrior named Caleb stepped up before his commander in chief. Before Joshua divided up any more land, Caleb provided a deed in the form of a promise guaranteeing the future home of Judah (Deut. 1:36).

Like a seasoned lawyer before the high court, Caleb presented his case in the form of a personal testimony. Commentator Donald Campbell notes:

> Caleb's life was ebbing away and he must make a choice. What did he still want most of all? In a remarkable address to Joshua he reviewed the highlights of his life and made his request. His brief autobiography highlighted events at Kadesh Barnea, during the wilderness wanderings, and the Conquest.[2]

His outline included three simple segments: his younger, middle, and later years.

The Younger Years

Caleb started his speech by reminding Joshua of one fateful day in the life of Israel:

> "You know the word which the Lord spoke to Moses the man of God concerning you and me in Kadesh-barnea. I was forty years old when Moses the servant of the Lord sent me from Kadesh-barnea to spy out the land, and I brought word back to him as it was in my heart. Nevertheless my brethren who went up with me made the heart of the people melt with fear; but I followed the Lord my God fully." (Josh. 14:6b–8)

Many years before, ten spies had quaked at the sight of giants

---

2. John F. Walvoord and Roy B. Zuck, *The Bible Knowledge Commentary* (Wheaton, Ill.: Scripture Press Publications, Inc., 1985.) Donald K. Campbell, "Joshua," The Bible Knowledge Commentary, Old Testament edition, ed. John F. Walvoord and Roy B Zuck (Wheaton, Ill.: Victor Books, 1985) p. 356.

occupying fortresses in the highest terrain of Canaan. Those spies looked in the mirror and saw themselves as grasshoppers (Num. 13:33). To Caleb, however, the giants were small because his God was large: "Caleb quieted the people before Moses and said, 'We should by all means go up and take possession of it, for we will surely overcome it'" (13:30). But ten swayed two million. Their cowardly report convinced a nation to abandon its faith and acquiesce to its fears (14:1–3).

The cowardly spies perished. The older generation died wandering in the desert. Only Joshua and Caleb, the two veterans, stood eye-to-eye. They were the only two left with scars from Pharaoh's shackles. Joshua no doubt remembered the promise made by Moses to this man of steely resolve:

> "So Moses swore on that day, saying, 'Surely the land
> on which your foot has trodden will be an inheritance
> to you and to your children forever, because you
> have followed the Lord my God fully.'" (Josh. 14:9)

When Israel turned its back on the Promised Land, Kadesh-barnea and the rest of southern Canaan remained in the control of the Anakim, led by the mythic-proportioned Arba (v. 15). In the hill country stood the city of Hebron, the highest and holiest point in Palestine.[3] The Hebron district encompassed Machpelah, the burial cave of Abraham, Sarah, and the patriarchs (Gen. 23:19; 49:30–31; 50:13). For Joshua, Hebron was the key to completing the conquest and receiving the blessing God intended for the Israelites. But the pervading question of the day was, "Who can stand before the sons of Anak?" (Deut. 9:2) In answer, an eighty-five-year-old relic flexed his muscles.

The Middle Years

Caleb continued:

> "Now behold, the Lord has let me live, just as He
> spoke, these forty-five years, from the time that the
> Lord spoke this word to Moses, when Israel walked
> in the wilderness; and now behold, I am eighty-five
> years old today." (Josh. 14:10)

---

3. F. F. Bruce, *New Bible Dictionary*, 2d ed., ed. J. D. Douglas and others (Wheaton, Ill.: Tyndale House Publishers, Inc., 1982), pp. 471–72.

Perhaps Caleb approached Joshua on his birthday. He believed Yahweh's hand sustained him all these years in anticipation of returning to the hill country. Caleb spent forty of his mid-life years wandering through desolation and five more years forcefully evicting the Canaanites. All that time, his eyes looked south to the hill country. Yet he never complained and never showed signs of bitterness. He simply waited for the green light. In fact, he viewed his long life as a gracious gift from God in spite of his uncomfortable circumstances:

> "I am still as strong today as I was in the day Moses sent me; as my strength was then, so my strength is now, for war and for going out and coming in." (v. 11)

You have to admire this man's spirit. His face weathered and wrinkled, Caleb still believed he could bench press what he did at forty. Caleb refused to let his situation decrease his vigor. Perhaps his long life was due in part to his determination to remain physically taut and battle ready. It's as if he never left that moment in Kadesh-barnea. This octogenarian never considered retirement, taking it easy, or perfecting his rocking chair rhythm. He trashed the "Gone Fishing" signs and raised his sword to lead the charge.

The Later Years

Caleb had hiked through that hill country in his younger years. He brought back a bunch of grapes as a foretaste of the future; the other spies experienced sour grapes instead. Caleb saw the same fortified cities as the other ten; he saw the same giants as the other ten; he saw the spears, the swords, the strength. But where the spies felt fear, Caleb found faith; where the spies cowered with terror, Caleb countered with courage. And when God ordered them to turn their backs from the Promised Land and the rolling hills of Hebron, Caleb waited quietly. Until now.

> "Now then, give me this hill country about which the Lord spoke on that day, for you heard on that day that Anakim were there, with great fortified cities; perhaps the Lord will be with me, and I will drive them out as the Lord has spoken." (v. 12)

Can you see his cheeks flush with passion? "Give me this hill country! Set me free, turn me loose, and with God's help I will have a villa overlooking the valley before sundown." Rather than slip quietly into old age and leave the heaviest fighting for young bucks, Caleb requested from Joshua the toughest assignment. Caleb laced up his hiking boots, strapped on his sword, and stood ready for his marching orders.

So Joshua blessed him and gave Hebron to Caleb
the son of Jephunneh for an inheritance. (v. 13)

Notice the position of Caleb, petitioning the commander in chief. While he appealed to the Mosaic promise, he recognized Yahweh's authority passed through Joshua. "Joshua blessed Caleb in the same manner as the patriarchal fathers blessed their sons ([see] Gen. 27; 24:60; 32:1)."[4] For forty-five years, Caleb had served behind the scenes as subordinate to his peer Joshua. He was just as brave, just as courageous, and just as worthy of the honor to lead, but for some unknown reason, Yahweh did not appoint Caleb. He wasn't even given the position of second in command.

Rather than whine, complain, or try to usurp Joshua's power, Caleb "followed the Lord God of Israel fully" (Josh. 14:14b). Caleb's walk with God far eclipsed his bravery. Again and again we hear this Hebrew phrase, "followed the Lord fully," as a refrain in the life of Caleb (Num. 14:24; 32:12; Deut. 1:36; Josh. 14:8, 9, 14). In fact, this phrase only appears one other time outside of the Caleb narratives. The writer of Kings used it to contrast how Solomon "did not follow the Lord fully," as his father David had done (1 Kings 11:6). David and Caleb—one a king, the other a warrior—were both passionate about pursuing God's own heart. And Caleb reaped God's rich rewards:

Therefore, Hebron became the inheritance of Caleb
the son of Jephunneh the Kenizzite until this day, because he followed the Lord God of Israel fully. . . .
Then the land had rest from war. (Josh. 14:14–15)

Caleb's attitude of fortitude convinced Joshua. Upon victory, Joshua decreed that the highest point in all of Palestine, Hebron, belonged to Caleb.

---

4. Trent C. Butler, "Joshua," in *Word Biblical Commentary*, vol. 7 (Dallas, Tex.: Word Books, Publisher, 1998.), vol. 7, accessed through the Logos Library System.

The young man who had stood confidently before the doubters clung to his youthful passion. Caleb, the man who elevated God's promise over his age, determined that retirement meant toppling fortified cities and achieving the impossible. Long before children gathered around the campfires and heard stories of a shepherd boy defeating the giant Goliath, they listened to the account of how aged Caleb felled three giants in his victory over the sons of Anakim (15:14).

Joshua 11:23 states, "Thus the land had rest from war." The conquest was complete for Joshua, and the people could now sheath their swords and harness their plows. Joshua 11:21–22 mentions that Israel finally defeated the dreaded Anakim. Often, Scripture mentions a fact and then elaborates on the details later. Though God created man in Genesis 1:27, He explained how He did it in Genesis 2. In this case, the author completed the summary of the conquest in Joshua 11 and then highlighted the hero in chapter 14. Chapter 14 concludes with the same comforting words of 11:23, "Thus the land had rest from war" (see v. 15). No doubt Caleb then retired to his mountain home—at least until God called him to lace up the hiking boots again!

Let's Take the Hill Country

Time to get up off the couch. Time to rethink retirement. It's time to find your own personal hill country and experience God's blessing regardless of your age. As you contemplate God's mission for your life, remember these three exhortations:

Forget your age. Your age is irrelevant.

> Ted Williams, at age 42 slammed a home run in his last official time at bat.

> Mickey Mantle, age 20, hit twenty-three home runs his first full year in the major leagues.

> Golda Meir was 71 when she became prime minister of Israel.

> William Pitt II was 24 when he became prime minister of Great Britain.

> George Bernard Shaw was 94 when one of his plays was first produced.

Mozart was just 7 when his first composition was published. . . .

Benjamin Franklin was a newspaper columnist at 16, and a framer of the United States Constitution when he was 81.[5]

God has bestowed upon you gifts, abilities, talents, and passions. In God's kingdom, you are never too young or too old to begin. Though you may have clocked in your hours for fifty years, believe it or not, your greatest life work may still be ahead of you. Similarly, though people may scoff at your youth, the Lord walks before you. If you have been using age as an excuse to avoid God's calling, you'd better find another one.

Focus on your goals. If you don't have any, find some! Caleb's eyes always diverted south to the hill country. What dreams have been buried under years of monotony or layers of insecurity? Set up some goals that are constantly before you—perhaps to disciple a neighbor or to start an overseas ministry. Don't allow time or age to be a deterrent. Keep those goals on the top of your mental list and pray about them consistently.

Follow your Lord fully. This was the refrain in Caleb's story. It was the foundation of his life and strength. Do you find yourself resentful for being passed over instead of being promoted? Have your dreams been clouded with aimlessness? Was your youth packed with potential, but now your middle age feels mired in mediocrity?

Caleb was faithful in his youth, yet he exchanged his dream for a forty-year hike. He was faithful even during years of aimless wandering. He served steadfastly under an equally gifted peer. The bottom line is that Caleb never allowed his circumstances to dictate his response to God. He always maintained a wholehearted passion for Yahweh. And in God's timing, not Caleb's, God granted Caleb the desires of his heart. Today the Lord still desires to exalt the faithful at the proper time.

Faithlessness could be defined as "fickle devotion through changing circumstances." Faithfulness could be defined as a "long obedience in the same direction regardless of the circumstances." Which one best describes you and your relationship with the Lord?

---

5. Chuck Swindoll, *The Tale of the Tardy Oxcart and 1,501 Other Stories* (Nashville, Tenn.: Word Publishing, 1998), pp. 28–29.

Living Insights

Age has never been an indicator of success. Scripture illustrates the irrelevance of age in God's kingdom. David felled Goliath as a teenager. Zecharias fathered John the Baptist when it was not thought medically possible. Josiah was eight years old when he became king and ruled righteously for thirty-one years. Paul, writing to young Timothy, exhorts him to not to look down upon his youth or to fear. "For God has not given us a spirit of timidity, but of power and love and discipline" (2 Tim. 1:7). The young seem to need courage to break free from insecurities and the old need courage to break out of lethargy. Forget your age for a minute. What task or passion has God given you? Put aside the excuses, put aside the insecurities, and tear up the "Gone Fishing" signs. God is not finished with you until He calls you home. Maybe you need to mentor a disadvantaged adolescent . . . Maybe you should start that ministry God placed upon your heart . . . Maybe you need to assemble an evangelistic prayer group.

Take a moment and write down all the excuses you have used in the past (money, age, fear, ridicule, and so on). Now, ask the Lord to remove these excuses from your life. Next, write down a prayer of commitment to pursue the passion God has given you:

My excuses: _____

_____

_____

_____

_____

My prayer: _____

_____

_____

_____

_____

✝ Invitation to Worship

Often, regardless of age, when we are asked to look back on life, we have a sense of regret. "What if . . ." "If I had only . . ." "My life has been a failure." Sovereignty is the belief that God is in control of all things, including the winding path of your life. God wastes nothing. He is grand enough to use every mishap, every victory, every circumstance, and every nuance of your life to impact others for His kingdom.

William Cowper wrote on the elusive subject of sovereignty:

> God moves in a mysterious way
> His wonders to perform;
> He plants His footsteps in the sea,
> And rides upon the storm.
>
> Deep in unfathomable mines
> Of never-failing skill
> He treasures up His bright designs,
> And works His sovereign will.
>
> Ye fearful saints, fresh courage take,
> The clouds ye so much dread
> Are big with mercy, and shall break
> In blessings on your head.[6]

Though the walk down memory lane might fill you with dread, His mercy shall break forth in new hope. Allow His beacon of light to burst through your darkened circumstances. Worship with the Psalmist:

> Yet I still belong to you;
> you are holding my right hand.
> You will keep on guiding me with your counsel,
> leading me to a glorious destiny.
> Whom have I in heaven but you?
> I desire you more than anything on earth.
> My health may fail, and my spirit may grow weak,
> but God remains the strength of my heart;
> he is mine forever. (Psalm 73:23–26 NLT)

6. As quoted by Paul Lee Tan, *Encyclopedia of 7,700 Illustrations* (Rockville, Md.: Assurance Publishers, 1979), no. 1938.

Chapter 16

GRACE AND TRUTH
WORTH REMEMBERING

Joshua 24:1–28

Their scars still fresh from opposing formidable Great Britain, the fledgling American colonies swelled with pride after their improbable victory. The infant nation was barely walking when Alexander Tyler uttered these prophetic warnings: "The average age of the world's greatest civilizations has been two hundred years. These nations have progressed through this sequence: from bondage to spiritual faith; from spiritual faith to great courage; from courage to liberty; from liberty to abundance; from abundance to complacency; from complacency to apathy; from apathy to dependence; from dependency back again into bondage."[1]

The nation of Israel was finally experiencing rest (Josh. 23:1). Dreams were fulfilled, desires were satisfied, and hopes were realized. The wanderers could finally worship in their new home. God desired the Israelites to cherish their abundance, reminding them: "'I gave you a land on which you had not labored, and cities which you had not built, and you have lived in them; you are eating of vineyards and olive groves which you did not plant'" (24:13). Formerly destitute nomads and wearied warriors, the Israelites could now feast on Yahweh's providence. They could stow their tents in the cellars of their new homes and tack their swords above the mantels. Israel had finally found rest.

Long before Alexander Tyler made his observations, Joshua pinpointed Israel's place in the cycle of nations, and predicted their doom if they allowed abundance to dull their allegiance to Yahweh. Abundance sidles up too closely to complacency. Rest teeters on the precipice of apathy. Joshua knew an insidious internal enemy prepared an ambush in the shadows of their external victories. He recognized that their toughest battle stood before them rather than behind them. But his time was running out.

---

1. Bryce Christensen, "The End of Patriotism: Tearing Up the Seedbed of the State," *The Family in America*, May 2000, vol. 14, no. 5; The Howard Center http://www.profam.org; as quoted on http://www.flash.net/~gregball/ largesse.htm, accessed January 11, 2002.

The Old Soldier Says Good-bye

General Lee affectionately addressed his troops after he signed the surrender at Appomattox. Departing military leaders possess an affinity for the faithful men who followed them through thick and thin. At the age of 110, General Joshua realized his time was short. Before he spoke to the populace, he gathered the leaders who had stood by him, his lieutenants who had executed his orders, this band of brothers who had endured the wilderness and evicted the Canaanites:

> Now it came about after many days, when the Lord had given rest to Israel from all their enemies on every side, and Joshua was old, advanced in years, that Joshua called for all Israel, for their elders and their heads and their judges and their officers, and said to them, "I am old, advanced in years." (23:1–2)

Chapter 23 recounts Joshua's speech to Israel's leaders. From it, we observe three significant attributes about Joshua. First, his wrinkles spoke of journeys long traveled and battles hard fought. "I am old, advanced in years." Rather than denying the reality of aging, he graciously welcomed it.

Secondly, despite his many victories and triumphs, he attributed any past success to the generous hand of God. "And you have seen all that the Lord your God has done to all these nations because of you, for the Lord your God is He who has been fighting for you" (v. 3, see also vv. 5, 9, 10). Joshua still possessed a good grasp of God's grace.

Thirdly, despite his old age, Joshua's passion reverberated with the idealism of youth. Hear his fervor when he admonished the leaders of Israel:

> "So be strong! Be very careful to follow all the instructions written in the Book of the Law of Moses. Do not deviate from them in any way. Make sure you do not associate with the other people still remaining in the land. Do not even mention the names of their gods, much less swear by them or worship them. But be faithful to the Lord your God as you have done until now. . . . So be very careful to love the Lord your God." (vv. 6–8, 11 NLT)

Old, but not outdated. Waning, but not weak. Close to death, but committed to life. Because Joshua was old, he had the people's respect. Because he had a grasp of grace, he possessed perspective on life. And because he had not lost his passion, he spoke with relevance. This man was not to be taken lightly.

> Then Joshua gathered all the tribes of Israel to Shechem, and called for the elders of Israel and for their heads and their judges and their officers; and they presented themselves before God. (24:1)

After addressing his executive staff, Joshua gathered all of Israel for a farewell speech. He might have been tempted to glory in his life's work and revel in Israel's successes. Eschewing sentimentality, he preached as if the task were just beginning. In his life, he had commanded his men to be strong and fight courageously against an entrenched enemy. Now, possibly days before his death, he beseeched them to fight on and root out an even more insidious enemy.

'Tis Grace Hath Brought Us Safe Thus Far

Joshua knew the people would become complacent if they forgot who secured their victory. So he started his speech with a refresher course on history:

> Joshua said to all the people, "Thus says the Lord, the God of Israel, 'From ancient times your fathers lived beyond the River, namely, Terah, the father of Abraham and the father of Nahor, and they served other gods. Then I took your father Abraham from beyond the River . . . led him . . . and multiplied his descendants and gave him Isaac. To Isaac I gave Jacob and Esau . . . Jacob and his sons went down to Egypt. Then I sent Moses and Aaron, and I plagued Egypt by what I did in its midst; and afterward I brought you out. I brought your fathers out of Egypt. . . . [I] put darkness between you and the Egyptians, and brought the sea upon them and covered them; and your own eyes saw what I did in Egypt. And you lived in the wilderness for a long time. Then I brought you into the land of the Amorites . . . and I gave them into your hand, and you took possession of their land when I destroyed them before you. Then Balak the son of Zippor, king of Moab, arose and fought against Israel . . . . and

I delivered you from his hand. I gave you a land on which you had not labored, and cities which you had not built, and you have lived in them; you are eating of vineyards and olive groves which you did not plant.'" (vv. 2–10, 13, emphasis added.)

Take a pen and underline the personal pronoun *I* in these verses. Notice a pattern? Without mincing words, Joshua left no doubt as to who was responsible for Israel's abundance: God. Joshua tells them, "Israel, pay attention. The bread you eat comes from grain you did not plant. Your hands did not build the house where your children play and lay their heads. Remember where your abundance comes from. Complacency will creep into your hearts unless you consistently and humbly acknowledge the unmerited blessings God has heaped upon you and your children."

Though the Lord provided rest from the swords of the Canaanites, the subtle seduction of Canaanite culture still pervaded the land. So Joshua turned from addressing the comfort of past glory to confronting present dangers.

Joshua Looks at the Present

Joshua knew that warriors were strengthened by battle and weakened by prosperity. Once the barricades were breached, the temptation was to become complacent, lethargic, and overconfident. Sheathing their swords did not mean letting down their guard, for the blessings of God were determined not by their military prowess, but their spiritual holiness. Trent Butler comments:

> "Rest is not the final word for life in the land. Temptation lurks in the presence of the gods of the peoples remaining in the land. Blessing can last only as long as total faithfulness to Yahweh lasts. When Israel begins to experiment with other gods, trying to be like the nations and worship every god possible, doom is imminent. Doom means loss of the promised and given land. Doom means aimless wandering, searching for a home like the ancient patriarchal father. Doom means destruction, death, disintegration of the people of God."[2]

2. Trent C. Butler, "Joshua," *Word Biblical Commentary* (Dallas, Tex.: Word Books, 1998), vol. 7, accessed through the Logos Library System.

So, as staunchly as Joshua had commanded them at the beginning of the conquest to "be strong and courageous" (Josh. 1:6a), he
charged them with a clear command and an essential choice. His
command was twofold:

> "Now, therefore, fear the Lord and serve Him in
> sincerity and truth; and put away the gods which
> your fathers served beyond the River and in Egypt."
> (24:14)

First, he commanded them to both fear and serve the Lord. *Fear*
involved a wholesome awe of God and a hatred of all the sin He
despised. *Serve* indicated a willing, sacrificial obedience based on
love and devotion. The first command spoke to Israel's heart; the
second command spoke to its will. Israel needed to prove its total
devotion to Yahweh. Some Israelites still secretly clung to Egyptian
gods toted through the wilderness. Some were "investigating" the
culture they just defeated. Joshua jarred them out of spiritual laxity.

Before Israel had a chance to say "Amen" or nod in agreement,
Joshua drew a line in the sand. He presented the Israelite people
with an essential choice:

> "If it is disagreeable in your sight to serve the Lord,
> choose for yourselves today whom you will serve:
> whether the gods which your fathers served which
> were beyond the River, or the gods of the Amorites
> in whose land you are living . . . ." (v. 15)

In essence, Joshua told them: "This isn't a cosmic buffet where
you choose the 'god of the day!' Your steadfast devotion does not
matter here; what matters is the *object* of your steadfast devotion.
Yahweh or not Yahweh. Not both/and. It is either/or. It is your
choice. You must choose today!"

As the people contemplated the depth of such a choice, Joshua
was the first to walk down the aisle:

> ". . . but as for me and my house, we will serve the
> Lord." (v. 15b)

Caught up in the emotional fervor of the moment, Israel echoed
with one voice:

> "Far be it from us that we should forsake the
> Lord to serve other gods . . . . We also will serve

the Lord, for He is our God." (vv. 16b, 18b)

At that moment, Joshua might have flashed back to another time when the Israelites made a similar pledge. At the foot of Mt. Sinai after Israel covenanted with Yahweh to wholeheartedly obey the Law, Joshua left with Moses to commune with God (Ex. 24:12–13). Less than two months later, he followed Moses down the mountain to discover that Israel had traded the glory of God to worship a golden calf (Ex. 32).

Joshua heard Israel's pledge and replied with a clarifying warning:

> "If you forsake the Lord and serve foreign gods, then
> He will turn and do you harm and consume you after
> He has done good to you." (Josh. 24:20)

But the people cried out again:

> "No, but we will serve the Lord." (v. 21b)

Like a judge asking a witness to certify the truth of his statements, Joshua pressed Israel once more to authenticate the covenant:

> Joshua said to the people, "You are witnesses against yourselves that you have chosen for yourselves the Lord, to serve Him." And they said, "We are witnesses." "Now therefore, put away the foreign gods which are in your midst, and incline your hearts to the Lord, the God of Israel." The people said to Joshua, "We will serve the Lord our God and we will obey His voice." (vv. 22–24)

A Memorial for the Future

> So Joshua made a covenant with the people that day, and made for them a statute and an ordinance in Shechem. . . . and he took a large stone and set it up there under the oak that was by the sanctuary of the Lord. Joshua said to all the people, "Behold, this stone shall be for a witness against us, for it has heard all the words of the Lord which He spoke to us; thus it shall be for a witness against you, so that you do not deny your God." (vv. 25–27)

Words fade from memory. Commitments made in elation are forgotten in temptation. However eloquent, however firm, however sincere, vows become distant, foggy memories. Joshua erected the stone to commemorate and stand as an everlasting witness of Israel's renewed covenant with Yahweh.[3]

Lessons Learned

Joshua recognized the bane of abundance—complacency eroding to apathy. People who have lost their dependence upon God will depend upon temporal things. Security, substances, and self-sufficiency become inadequate rulers who try to depose the Sovereign Lord in our lives. Take some time to reflect as Joshua did. Peer into the past, pause in the present, and commit to the future.

When you look back to the past, see God's grace and be grateful for it. Regardless of your present circumstances, if you have put your trust in Christ, you have experienced the grace of God. Unaided, the Lord bestowed the unmerited, unearned gift of His son's death so that you might live. Survey the twist and turns of your life's journey. Focus your lens on those places where your footprints disappeared as He carried you mercifully along through the toils and trials of life. Remember the undeserved blessings He lavished. Be grateful.

When you look at the present, hear God's truth and be challenged by it. God's truth casts light into the shadows of our hearts. Encouraging and convicting, His Word both provides comfort and rebukes carnal tendencies. Even now, the Holy Spirit might be prodding you to step up and confess an addiction, an idol, a misguided deed, or a wrong motive. Hebrews 4:12 states: "For the word of God is living and active and sharper than any two-edged sword, and piercing as far as the division of soul and spirit, of both joints and marrow, and able to judge the thoughts and intentions of the heart." He speaks to believers today through His word and by the power of the Holy Spirit. He is waiting with open arms to receive your confession and affirm your commitment to live for Him.

When you look into the future, remember your commitment and be strengthened because of it. Where is your covenant stone? When were those moments when you abandoned reason, or fear, or reputation and pledged allegiance to Him only? As you contemplate decisions,

---

3. Donald Campbell notes, "Archeologists excavating the site of Shechem have uncovered a great limestone pillar which may be identified with the memorial referred to here." Campbell, "Joshua," *The Bible Knowledge Commentary*, Old Testament edition, ed. John F. Walvoord and Roy B. Zuck (Wheaton, Ill.: Victor Books, 1985), p. 370.

life goals, and how your life will look in the future, revisit those sanctified commitments. Wanderers lean upon their own understanding. Worshipers trust in the Lord's statutes to straighten crooked paths.

 Living Insights

Two burials. Two crises. One nation, two antithetical responses. We've taken time to look at the last few chapters of Joshua. The book ends with the honorable death of the faithful Israelite leader and with a crisis, a leadership transition. Israel responds in faith and obedience. The book of Joshua closes with the words: "Israel served the Lord all the days of Joshua and all the days of the elders who survived Joshua" (24:31).

Now take some time to read the last few chapters of the very next book in Scripture. Judges ends with a grisly death—the dismemberment of the Levite's concubine—and a crisis—the possible extinction of the tribe of Benjamin. As the priests of Yahweh cavorted with prostitutes and the nation teetered on chaos, Israel's response signified weeds had already claimed the stone in Shechem. Judges closes with "In those days there was no king in Israel; *everyone did what was right in his own eyes*" (21:25, emphasis added).

One book and about three hundred years removed from Joshua's legacy,[4] Israel had long forgotten the allegiance made to Yahweh at Shechem. Once worshipers, they now found themselves wandering again in the muddied quagmire of indifference and disobedience. Once freed by God's grace, the Israelites now stood as prisoners shackled to selfishness. They lost their direction and more importantly, their commitment.

Our commitments often need renewal notices. Otherwise, in our abundance, complacency seduces our hearts. Devotion to Almighty God reduces to an afterthought, and our selfish pursuits supplant our spiritual passions.

---

4. "Since most scholars agree that the monarchy began under Saul in 1051 B.C., the debate centers on Joshua's death. . . . The evidence for beginning the period of the Judges about 1350 B.C. is strong . . . ." Thus the time period would be about three hundred years. F. Duane Lindsey, "Judges," *The Bible Knowledge Commentary*, Old Testament edition, ed. John F. Walvoord and Roy B. Zuck (Wheaton, Ill.: Victor Books, 1985), p. 373.

Return to your "Shechem." Clear out the weeds surrounding the covenant stone. Listen to words spoken long ago pledging your sole devotion to the Lord. Invite Him to change your wanderings into worship.

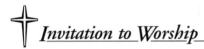 *Invitation to Worship*

> Through many dangers, toils and snares,
> I have already come;
> 'Tis grace hath brought me safe thus far,
> And grace will lead me home.[5]

The wanderers toiled through four hundred years of slavery. The wanderers trudged through the many snares of the wilderness. They came through the sea and through the armies. Grace sustained them; grace led them home. You may be toiling. You may be wandering through the snares of the enemy, of pain, of disappointment, of sin. Grace sustains you. Grace will lead you home.

Even in your wanderings, you experience the grace of God. He is the hope when hope seems dim. During a "wandering" time in your life, follow the example of the wandering Israelites. Though destitute, they devoted themselves to Yahweh; though wandering in the land, they worshiped the Lord. The tabernacle reminded them that their focus was to be on the presence of the Lord, not on their ever-present problems. If you are a believer, you have His Spirit within your tabernacle, your body. How much closer His presence is to you. Take a few moments to thank Him for His closeness. Praise Him by singing, "Amazing grace! how sweet the sound . . . ."

5. John Newton, "Amazing Grace," in *Worship and Service Hymnal* (Hope Publishing Company, 1957), no. 226.

BOOKS FOR
PROBING FURTHER

W e have reached the end of our long journey from the land of Egypt to the Promised Land. God's covenant love for His chosen people was evident every step of the way as He led His people out of bondage and into a land flowing with milk and honey.

We pray that as you have walked with the Israelites through the wilderness, you have discovered some meaningful truths about God's character, provision, and promises. Hopefully, you have also learned to become a more obedient and reverent worshiper of Him.

To provide you with the opportunity to explore this topic more deeply, we are recommending the following books. As you continue your travels through the Christian life, we hope these books will make the road more smooth and the journey more refreshing.

Bright, John. *A History of Israel.* Philadelphia, Penn.: Westminster Press, 1981.

Brueggemann, Walter. *Israel's Praise: Doxology Against Idolatry and Ideology.* Minneapolis, Minn.: Fortress Press, 1988.

Dillard, Raymond B. and Tremper Longman III. *An Introduction to the Old Testament.* Grand Rapids, Mich.: Zondervan Publishing House, 1994.

Gaebelein, Frank E., gen. ed. *The Expositor's Bible Commentary.* Volumes 2 and 3. Grand Rapids, Mich: Zondervan Publishing House, 1992.

Hoffmeier, James K. *Israel in Egypt: The Evidence for the Authenticity of the Exodus Tradition.* Oxford, England: Oxford University Press, 1999.

Nelson's Complete Book of Bible Maps and Charts: Old and New Testaments. Nashville, Tenn.: Thomas Nelson Publishers, 1982.

Peterson, Eugene. *The Message: The Old Testament Books of Moses.* Colorado Springs, Colo.: NavPress, 2001.

Sailhamer, John. *The Pentateuch as Narrative.* Grand Rapids, Mich.: Zondervan Publishing House, 1992.

Sarna, Nahum. *Exploring Exodus: The Origins of Biblical Israel*. New York, N.Y.: Schocken Books, 1996.

Swindoll, Charles. *Moses: A Man of Selfless Dedication*. Nashville, Tenn.: Word Publishing, 1999.

Tullock, John H. *The Old Testament Story*. Englewood Cliffs, N.J.: Prentice Hall, 1981.

Zornberg, Avivah Gottlieb. *The Particulars of Rapture: Reflections on Exodus*. New York, N.Y.: Doubleday, 2001.

Some of the books listed may be out of print and available only through a library. For those currently available, please contact your local Christian bookstore. Books by Charles R. Swindoll may be obtained through the Insight for Living Resource Center, as well as many books by other authors. Just call the IFL office that serves you.

Insight for Living also has Bible study guides available on many books of the Bible as well as on a variety of topics, Bible characters, and contemporary issues. For more information, see the ordering instructions that follow and contact the office that serves you.

ORDERING INFORMATION

CHANGING WANDERERS INTO WORSHIPERS

If you would like to order additional Bible study guides, purchase the audiocassette series that accompanies this guide, or request our product catalogs, please contact the office that serves you.

United States and International locations:

Insight for Living
Post Office Box 269000
Plano, TX 75026-9000

1-800-772-8888, 24 hours a day, seven days a week (U.S. contacts) International constituents may contact the U.S. office through mail queries.

Canada:

Insight for Living Ministries
Post Office Box 2510
Vancouver, BC, Canada V6B 3W7

1-800-663-7639, 24 hours a day, seven days a week
insight.canada@insight.org

Australia:

Insight for Living, Inc.
20 Albert Street
Blackburn, VIC 3130, Australia

Toll-free 1800 772 888 or (03) 9877-4277, 8:30 A.M. to 5:00 P.M., Monday to Friday
iflaus@insight.org

Internet:

www.insight.org

Bible Study Guide Subscription Program

Bible study guide subscriptions are available. Please call or write the office nearest you to find out how you can receive our Bible study guides on a regular basis.